SOUL
searching

MEDITATIONS *for* YOUR SPIRITUAL JOURNEY

A
JANET
THOMA
BOOK

Thomas Nelson Publishers

Nashville • Atlanta • London • Vancouver

Published in Nashville, Tennessee, by Thomas Nelson, Inc., Publishers, and distributed in Canada by Word Communications, Ltd., Richmond, British Columbia.

The Bible version used in this publication is THE NEW KING JAMES VERSION. Copyright © 1979, 1980, 1982, 1990 Thomas Nelson, Inc., Publishers.

Library of Congress Cataloging-in-Publication Data

Soul searching : meditations for your spiritual journey.
        p.   cm.
    Originally published as a 4 vol. set, Seasons of life meditations, 1994.
    Contents: Spring / Anne Christian Buchanan — Summer / Bernie Sheahan — Autumn / Catharine Walkinshaw — Winter / Debra Klingsporn.
    ISBN 0-7852-7718-8
    1. Seasons—Religious aspects—Christianity.   2. Meditations.
I. Buchanan, Anne Christian.   Spring.   II. Sheahan, Bernie.
Summer.   III. Walkinshaw, Catharine.   Autumn.   IV. Klingsporn, Debra.   Winter.
BV4800.S63   1995
242'.2—dc20   95-19271
                                                             CIP

Printed in the United States of America
1 2 3 4 5 6 — 00 99 98 97 96 95

CONTENTS

. . . .

To everything there is a season,
A time for every purpose under heaven:
A time to be born,
And a time to die;
A time to plant,
And a time to pluck what is planted;
A time to kill,
And a time to heal;
A time to break down,
And a time to build up;
A time to weep,
And a time to laugh;
A time to mourn,
And a time to dance;
A time to cast away stones,
And a time to gather stones;
A time to embrace,
And a time to refrain from embracing;
A time to gain,
And a time to lose;
A time to keep,
And a time to throw away;
A time to tear,
And a time to sew;
A time to keep silence,
And a time to speak;
A time to love,
And a time to hate;
A time of war,
And a time of peace.

Ecclesiastes 3:1–8

. . . .

To Everything There Is a Season

The seasons of life are more than spring, summer, fall, and winter. There is a season when you prepare for childbirth, and a season for saying goodbye to a loved one. There is the season of working hard for financial security, and there is the season of smelling roses and walking hand in hand with a loved one.

A season is not defined as much by an increment of time or the changing landscape as it is by a lesson learned or wisdom gained. And with each new season you will need a new set of skills and strengths. You will need endurance to face childbirth, and understanding to help you grieve a loss. Patience and determination will be essential as you climb the corporate ladder, and peace and joy will accompany you as you walk with your partner through all the fields of life.

Soul Searching was created to be a friend traveling with you as you experience the joys and sorrows of each season. It will console, energize, counsel, chide, and inspire. These meditations contain the gentle wisdom of those who have experienced many seasons of their own. While they may not completely understand your situation, the authors have been somewhere similar and can offer advice to help you understand yourself, your emotions, God, and your world.

The authors and editors wish you peace, wisdom, and love as you face all of your seasons of life.

S O U L
searching

WINTER

a time for peace

. . . .

*This book is lovingly dedicated to Betty,
who is living the seasons of her life with grace;
Gary, who has seen me through
the winters of my faith;
Katy, who is sunshine incarnate;
and Kari, who is grace revisited.*

. . . .

She wanted to be a princess. Nothing less would do. So out came the dust-covered sewing machine, and following a few late nights of mother-turned-seamstress, she stepped into her fantasy that had been brought to life. A deep, rich purple princess gown, with a luminescent metallic weave, royal gold cape, and diamond tiara—she was going to be a trick-or-treater of bedazzling beauty. She awaited Halloween that year with greater anticipation than Christmas. Trick-or-treating in her princess costume was going to be the *big event*.

Mother Nature had other plans.

We awoke that morning to find the first few inches of an early snowfall. No problem. In Minnesota, a couple of inches of snow isn't enough to halt determined trick-or-treaters.

But the snow kept coming. Not just an early dusting, but a full-scale, record-breaking blizzard. By early afternoon the snow was over a foot deep with drifts nearing two feet. And the snow kept coming. By evening, travel advisories kept people off the roads. Halloween was going to come and go that year without the traditional neighborhood trick-or-treating. The storm, known as the "Halloween Blizzard," broke all records, scrambled all plans, backed up traffic, and brought everything to an overnight halt.

Winter came early but my little princess was undaunted. She went on enjoying the moment for exactly what it was—a once-in-a-lifetime adventure—playing in the snow wearing her luminescent princess costume accessorized with snow boots, mittens, and jacket.

I was prepared for disappointment; she greeted the blizzard with anticipation. I was aware of hazards; she was ready for hot chocolate and marshmallows. I was unwilling for winter to come so soon; she was dancing around asking for her sled and boots.

Motorists weren't the only ones blinded by the blizzard. I, too, had to look twice. Sometimes we see clearly through the eyes of another what we miss on our own.

Lord, make me see.

*Certain words need to be taken out of
disuse, dusted off, and heard anew.*
—*D. K. Klingsporn*

*C*ertain words have long been worn out for me.
I hear them spoken and automatically my mind
shifts into the "ignore mode," something like the
screen dimmer software on my computer that turns
my computer screen to fireworks after a period of
inactivity. *Salvation* is one of those words. It even
sounds old.

Salvation. Frederick Buechner says, "It is a process, not an event."[1] I find that disconcerting. I want
an event, something like Christmas. I want a grand
and glorious once-and-for-all event.

This God of seasons and stages, life and death,
cold and warmth; this God of contrasts and para-
dox; this is not a God of easy answers and ready
reassurance. I want a once-and-for-all god. The
kind that makes you go through something once,
and you don't have to go through it again. Once
you've tasted the salty sting from tears of grief, you
can dry your eyes, blow your nose and say, "Okay,
God, I've done that once. I don't have to do that
again." I want the kind of faith that once you figure
out what *it* is, you don't have to keep wrestling with
it. The kind that once you say, "Okay, God, I'll give

you my life," you don't have to keep learning what giving it to him actually means.

Yet that worn-out, frumpy word *salvation* keeps coming back to mind. Other words are much more popular and more stylish during the Christmas season—like peace, hope, and joy. But those words don't save me from myself. From my temper, or my self-centered, impatient tendencies. They don't save me from my preference to control, not only my life, but also everyone around me.

So I come to this word, this God who stages an event that transforms the world, wanting the transformation of me to be a once-and-for-all. But it never will be, because life itself is so daily. If I had salvation or faith or God Himself, once-and-for-all, I would probably forget it (or him) tomorrow. I can only live this one day and experience the saving grace of God within this present moment.

Salvation. A process, not an event, that daily saves me from myself. Perhaps it isn't such a worn-out word after all.

Now faith is the substance of things hoped
for, the evidence of things not seen.
—*Hebrews 11:1*

I grew up on the Gulf coast where ice was something that accompanied cold beverages, snow was something pictured by Courier & Ives, and temperatures below freezing were a once-a-winter occurrence. Winter was simply a milder version of the preceding months; a little more rain, a little more fog, and an occasional opportunity to wear a sweater or a coat.

Then we moved to Minnesota. Rolling farmland, magnificent trees, sparkling lakes—and long, long winters. After weathering a few, I learned there are actually two winters: one pre-holidays and one post-New Year's. The winter of November and December is a season of anticipation, a welcome change. A time to pull out knee socks and wool sweaters. A time to decorate for family gatherings. A time of cozy evenings and anticipated events. Winter One, the holiday winter, is festive, invigorating, full of promise and excitement.

Then comes Winter Two. Post-New Year's Day. Weeks of sub-zero windchills, dark days, colorless grays, and dirty snow. The beauty of the season's first snowfall is long forgotten with the aggravation of icy sidewalks, numb fingers, and cold toes.

Winter One and Winter Two are back to back contrasts. One is a celebration; the other is an endurance test. One is a season of vibrance; the other a season of dormancy.

Long winters experienced in two stages may be a phenomenon of the upper midwest, but contrasts of the heart are universal. We experience the same surroundings, the same relationships, the same career as Winter One and Winter Two. One day is vibrant, the next day dormant. What we too often fail to recognize is the value of the dormant phase, a time of invisible happenings. To embrace the Winter Two of our hearts is to embrace a necessary time of unseen renewal, of new beginnings yet to come. The startling beginnings of new life always follow the darkness of a dormant season.

God, see me through the days my life feels dormant. When I feel like nothing's happening, reassure my impatient heart that you are present in every season of life.

If you get simple beauty and naught else,
You get about the best thing God invents.
—Robert Browning

Hot chocolate and wet mittens. Snowballs and sledding. A downhill ski run on fresh powder. A wonderland of white. Winter—picturesque and poignant.

Yet I grew up in South Texas where winter provided merely a brief interval from summer's heat, Christmas was accompanied by the hum of air conditioners, and we were actually excited to have an opportunity to wear sweaters! Nonetheless, visions of ice skating on frozen ponds, colorful mufflers, frosty windowpanes and white Christmases still define my image of winter, as they do for many of us. Yet my day-to-day experience of winter in Minnesota is at odds with the poet's portrayal of winter's serene beauty.

I could easily rename winter as the season of layers and distractions. Contending with coats, wet shoes, and commutes made longer by nasty weather. Why is it that life seems more bothersome, more complicated in the winter? Simply getting out the door with all the necessary winter gear proves challenging: coat, gloves, hat. Oh, where are my keys? Should I take my umbrella?

Winter. A season of layers. A season of distractions. Instead of welcoming a season of quiet stillness and poetic beauty, I contend with winter's chaos and the adult aggravations of feet that can't get warm, cars that won't start, and flu medicine that doesn't help.

Opening myself to the wonders of this season comes only when I shed the layers of adult thinking that blind me to a season of magic. Usually my fits of frustration are directly proportional to my level of overcommitment, anxiety, and stress. What may be an aggravation one day can provide comic relief another. The difference is within me, not in the situation. When I'm blind to the season's beauty, I need to ask myself *What are the unnecessary layers that bind me? Is my life too cluttered right now?*

Life is too short to miss the beauty and magic of any season. Today I'm going to come out from under the layers of cluttered thinking and seek the simple beauty around me.

Each of us tends to be, not a single self,
but a whole committee of selves.
— *Thomas Kelly*

*W*inter's return is synonymous with the return
of hats. Rain hats. Snow hats. Felt hats. Knit hats.
Even those who dislike hats have at least a few for
the winter months. Our hats are as interchangeable
as our roles, and no other month calls upon or
combines more of them than December.

How many hats do I wear? How many roles do
I play? Mother, daughter, wife, hostess, shopper,
cook, planner, keeper of the bank card, spender of
the kingdom.

The number of hats I wear the rest of the year
seems to multiply geometrically in December. In the
pull and tug of overlapping roles and responsibilities, we can lose touch with the woman within: the
dreamer, the lover, the poet, the adventurer, the
child. More than four decades ago, Anne Morrow
Lindbergh wrote, "I must try to be alone for part
of each year, even a week or a few days; and for
part of each day, even for an hour or a few minutes
in order to keep my core, my center."

Who am I at my core, my center? Who am I apart
from my roles? Am I so married to the demands of
my day that to pull away even for an hour or a few

minutes is an opportunity for guilt to run rampant? If the hats we wear rule our lives, we are committing a gradual suicide of self, with the "committee of selves" clamoring for a singleness of purpose.

We are more than a composite of the roles we fulfill. To stay in touch with the woman within is to enrich the roles we assume. Richard Foster, author of *Celebration of Discipline,* says the early church fathers spoke of *Otium Sanctum,* or *holy leisure,* an ability to pace ourselves, to rest and be at peace through the activities of the day. "We must pursue 'holy leisure' with a determination that is ruthless to our datebooks,"[2] Foster writes. Good words to remember: holy leisure. The more demanding our roles, the more essential is time to ourselves.

Time to myself is a necessity, not a luxury. With a determination that is ruthless to my datebook, I will make time for holy leisure.

*Your only safety is to be within the center
of your kingdom, living from within out,
not from without in.*

—*Mary Strong*

*T*like watching elderly ladies who have lived
their lives in the harsh winters of the upper midwest.
They wear clunky boots, bulky coats, unbecoming
hats. Their concern is not for vanity, but rather for
comfort. They seem indifferent to making a fashion
statement. They know what works to cut winter's
chill—and that's of much greater importance to
them than appearance. Their coats have withstood
many seasons' snowfalls. Their shoes are well-worn
and warm.

There's something of a ritual to the order of donning their winter apparel. Muffler first, tied just so,
coat next, always buttoned up to the neck, then
gloves and hat. In that order, and only at one speed.
You can't hurry the elderly just like you can't hurry
a child. They have two gears: stop and go. They
live according to an inner clock, a timetable of their
own keeping, seldom flustered by external demands. The ritual for donning or relinquishing winter apparel remains the same, no matter how you
try to hurry or "encourage" them.

I, on the other hand, wear shoes that make my

feet ache—because they look better. I'll go without a coat, because it doesn't look right. I'll rush my kids because I'm running late, but I tell them, "We're late!" I allow my day, my choices, my mood to be determined by the externals: the pressures, demands, obligations, and expectations.

In *Telling Secrets* author Frederick Buechner quotes from the *Letters from the Scattered Brotherhood*, "You're only safety is to be within the center of your kingdom, living from within out, not from without in."[3]

Elderly ladies who listen to an inner clock, who move at their own pace wearing clunky boots, bulky coats, and unbecoming hats, know something of what it means to live from "within out," rather than from "without in." Living from within out means defining who I am from within, rather than allowing circumstances, expectations, or fears to become the essence of who I am.

Learning to live from within out is an art, a skill, something I may not do well or consistently right now, but something I can learn nonetheless.

 *Let me live this day from within out rather than living from without in, learning to define who I am from an inner source.*

*Begin where you are. Live this present
moment . . . keep up a silent prayer,
"Open thou my life. Guide my
thoughts . . . Thy will be done."*
                                    —Thomas Kelly

With the first cold weather comes the unmistakable wispy puffs of white—our breath as it hits the cold air.

We are often too busy to notice. Something we see every winter season, like early morning frost or the smell of wood burning in neighboring fireplaces, our little puffs of visible air are reminders that the simple act of breathing is life itself.

A simple breath of air—a cloud formed and quickly dissipated. A child's fascination with the condensation formed by breathing on frosty windowpanes. Reminders that are easily ignored and easily lost in our dismissal of the insignificant. Yet these little momentary cloud formations are visible reminders that I'm alive. This day might not have been—but it is. I might not be experiencing what I have before me—but I am. Whatever awaits me in this day, I am alive. I may greet the day with anticipation or dread, but I am alive.

*Today, God, I celebrate the gift of life.
Open my life and my heart to the fullness
of the moment.*

The angel said to her, "Rejoice, highly favored one, the Lord is with you: blessed are you among women!" But when she saw him, she was troubled at his saying, and considered what manner of greeting this was. Then the angel said to her, "Do not be afraid, Mary, for you have found favor with God."

—Luke 1:28–29

I believe in angels. No formal theology to explain it—no proof. I just like the image of an invisible presence dropping in unannounced at times I'm least aware.

Angels, and reports of their appearance, have been around for as long as history has been recorded; they're not exclusive to the Judeo-Christian tradition.

Yet the Judeo-Christian tradition is a rich reservoir for the angel-seeker in us all. "For He shall give His angels charge over you, / To keep you in all your ways," writes the psalmist in Psalm 91:11. Ezekiel, one of the Old Testament prophets wrote, "Behold, I send an Angel before you to keep you in the way and to bring you into the place which I have prepared." Considering that prophets were notoriously unpopular, if anyone needed someone watching over them, they did!

But without a doubt, probably the angel we are most familiar with is Gabriel, the one who approached Mary to inform her about plans for a Christ child, a child she would bear.

Abbie Jane Wells says, "For all I know—for all anybody knows—God may have 'proposed' (or propositioned?) . . . through the ages, but as far as we know, Mary was the first one to say an unqualified 'yes.'"[4]

Mary said yes to an angel, and her name has been holy ever since.

I guess we could conclude that saying yes to angels (or God as it were) can take our lives in directions we would never dream, but have you ever considered how different Mary's life would have been if she had said no? Her greatest joys, her deepest longings, her place in history would have never been.

When I'm approached by holy propositions, unexpected messengers, or angels in 20th century disguise, am I willing to respond with an unqualified yes? By the grace of God, I hope so.

Lord, let me not reject holy propositions, unlikely messengers, or risky opportunities for fear of the possible consequences.

Create in me a clean heart, O God,
And renew a steadfast spirit within me.
—Psalm 51:10

"*D*on't buy a house with a long driveway."

Such was the advice we received from friends when we arrived in Minnesota. Strange advice that was quickly forgotten in our frenzied hunt for a house.

Yes, we did buy a house with a long driveway. After only one Minnesota winter and seventy inches of snow later, we remembered the advice and understood the wisdom.

Not wanting to waste time with the unnecessary, we didn't shovel much that first winter. The snowfalls weren't *that* deep—only three or four inches at a time. Our cars could easily pack the snow down and we could get in and out of the driveway. Why bother?

Then came the mid-winter thaws, those brief respites from the severe temperatures when the sun shone and temperatures rose to the high twenties or above. Our rock-solid, snow-packed driveway thawed to slush, and then froze again as temperatures plummeted overnight. Over and over the thawing and freezing continued until our driveway was a slippery, treacherous collage of ice ruts.

After one winter we had learned our lesson. Tend to the shoveling as the snow falls—remedial snow and ice removal is far more difficult than shoveling the fresh stuff.

So it is with our work of the heart. Hurts, resentments, daily disappointments seldom come with blizzard-like intensity. They more often start small and are easily ignored: an incident here, a thoughtless word there.

I'll deal with this later, we say to ourselves as we minimize the hurt, the anger, the misunderstanding.

But the accumulation can be deadly, freezing the joy and passion from our lives as our heart is warmed and chilled in succession. Daily tending to matters of the heart is essential: letting go of the resentments we harbor by putting them in God's hands; shoveling out from under the confusion of anger by talking with a trusted friend; keeping the build-up to a minimum by journaling, praying, or seeking the counsel of another. These are only a few of the shovels God gives us.

Offering apologies. Speaking an honest word. Confronting an injustice. These are much like shoveling snow. They keep the way clear and prevent slippery missteps.

There's no limit to how complicated things can get, on account of one thing always leading to another.

—E. B. White

I frequently take walks in a wildlife preserve not far from my home. The paved path winds through a wooded area, along a marsh, and around a small lake. As I walk my familiar route, the landscape of winter is one of barren branches. No leaves or undergrowth block the view, only skeletal trees in varying shades of grays and sepia tones. The bramble of twigs and limbs obscures, but never completely blocks, my view of the winter landscape. The barrenness of winter provides a clarity all its own.

So to with silence. Despite the incessant lists of things to do, I feel something within me calling me away from "doing" to seek the clarity of silence. Yet the stillness of winter's silence is uncomfortable. Despite being a seeker of God all my life, I still wrestle with an inner resistance to embrace the quiet. Frenetic doing comes much more easily. I readily turn my attention to the demand of bills to pay, checkbook to balance, errands to run, and phone calls to return. Give me tasks with a finite beginning and ending, then I'm in my element. But to walk willingly into the silence, the barrenness of my inner self, is a daunting task.

Busyness begets busyness. One thing leads to another. Picking up an empty coffee cup and taking it to the kitchen leads me to unload the dishwasher, leads me to take out the trash, leads me to an unending awareness of more that needs to be done. And in the busyness, I seldom see the holy. I seldom hear the gentle voice calling me from within, *Be still and know that I am God*.

Ignoring the empty coffee cup, unplugging the phone from the wall, and allowing myself to sit in the disquieting silence is to give myself an opportunity for grace to happen. The uncomfortable silence gives way to a presence. For it is only in the quiet that I can hear God's word of healing and hope. God doesn't compete with my busyness; he waits patiently until I'm ready to see, to hear, to welcome the barren clarity of honesty with myself and my maker.

Winter's silence has a clarity all its own. Today I will seek a simplicity of the heart.

We have this moment . . .
— *Gloria Gaither*

I've always loved snow globes, those miniature winter scenes enclosed in a plastic or glass covering with snowflakes floating in a clear liquid. When shaken or turned upside down, the scenes come to life with swirling snow. Snow globes come as intricate, expensive music boxes or the cheap discount store variety, which was the kind we always found in our Christmas stockings.

Sitting on my kitchen windowsill is a different kind of snow globe. Enclosed in the small, upright cylinder is the customary clear liquid with a miniature black top hat floating on the top, a tiny carrot, and five small black buttons. Across the bottom is the inscription "Texas Snowman." No snowflakes swirl in this snow globe. Turn it upside down or shake it vigorously, and all that swirls are the remaining parts of the melted snowman: a top hat, a carrot nose, two charcoal eyes, and three charcoal buttons.

A snowman in Texas, if an occasional snowstorm makes one possible at all, can't last. The odds are against him. The sun will surely come out, the temperatures will rise, and the snowman inevitably will turn into a puddle.

I love the whimsy and humor of my "Texas Snowman." I find that it helps my perspective to take a good hard look at it some days. I'm reminded that even when the odds are against it, something beautiful and unexpected *can* happen, even if ever so briefly. I'm reminded that some of the best things in life can't last forever. And I'm reminded that wanting something or someplace or someone to be something they aren't will surely result in my missing the momentary, miraculous, whimsy of the moment I have before me. Nothing closes my heart to the present more effectively than wishing the present were different. And probably most important of all, my "Texas Snowman" reminds me to laugh.

No matter where I am, no matter what obstacles I'm facing, I will seek the laughter in my winter.

I wait for the LORD, my soul waits,
And in His word I do hope.
My soul waits for the LORD
More than those who watch for the
*   morning.*

—Psalm 130:5–6

*C*old days. Long nights. December. A season of waiting. Waiting for the first cup of coffee to brew on a cold, dreary morning. Waiting for clouds to clear. Waiting for the first snowfall after the ground has turned brown. Waiting for the holidays with the newspaper daily reminding me how many shopping days are left until Christmas.

I've never been very patient with waiting. In fact, I hate to wait. I fume when placed on hold by a reservations clerk. I feel the tension creeping in my shoulders when waiting for slow-moving traffic on slick, wet roads. Whether waiting for a doctor's appointment or waiting in a grocery checkout line, I like things to happen *now*.

So the phrase "wait on the Lord" has always been a bit baffling to me. Why? What exactly was the psalmist waiting for?

The psalmist knew something I'm only now beginning to appreciate—waiting implies promise. We don't wait for something unless there's something we're waiting for. We don't wait for Christmas, unless Christmas means something to us. We don't wait in traffic, unless there's somewhere we want to go. If we didn't drink coffee, we wouldn't wait for the coffee to brew.

Waiting on the Lord is acknowledging God's timing, not ours. Waiting on the Lord is giving up our need to control, to make things happen. Waiting on the Lord is anticipating God's acting in our lives. Waiting on the Lord is faith.

Waiting on the Lord, even when we sometimes don't know exactly what we are waiting for, is what faith is all about.

How can I sing a song of the hills,
Bare hills under skies of gray?
How can I sing when the leaves lie dead,
And the flowers have been called away?
How can I sing?

—Bula E. Legg

*A*nother gray, dreary day. Wind, rain, sleet, snow. Ah, the variety of ways the weather can dampen my spirits. The overcast skies rob the color from my world and I feel alone. Gray days feel like Mondays—days full of too much to do and too little time. Days with responsibilities crowding in and joy crowded out. Gray days.

Yet in the road are dancing leaves. Leaves swirling in circular patterns across the street. Dancing leaves, you dance in circles, going nowhere in particular. Don't you know today is bitter and cold? Don't you realize the wind is making your world an unfriendly place? Under gray skies and nasty weather, today is a day of overcoats pulled tight and hats pulled low. The frost of winter's chill seems to freeze what little warmth we might offer each other on any other kind of day.

Still you dance. Crusty brown leaves, wrinkled and lifeless, you dance. Yet this dance is not your own. Left to your own volition, you'd be sitting in the nearest compost pile. No, this dance of yours comes from a source completely other than your ring of swirling leaves. This dance of yours is a defiant one, a dance which laughs at the melancholy gray.

Perhaps this wind can blow a dance into my lifeless heart today. If I but take a deep, deep breath, close my eyes and open my heart, I can feel the dance within. Slowly, slowly, the song returns, and I know I can see beyond the gray. Dancing leaves, your defiance is contagious.

> Spirit of the living God,
> Surround my dreary world today
> And set my feet to dancing.
> The silent song of days gone gray,
> A heart that's heavy laden,
> Won't have the last, the final say.
> I know a song of dancing leaves,
> They swirl and twirl despite the gray.
> Spirit of the living God,
> Set my feet to dancing.[5]

Spirit of the living God, set my feet to dancing.

*God often gives in one brief moment that
which he has for a long time denied.*
—*Thomas Kempis*

*O*ur second daughter was born amid fears and
uncertainties. In the eighth month of pregnancy, a
routine ultrasound detected a growth problem. The
medical tests and the neonatologists could only tell
us what was *not* wrong. Nobody could tell us what
was wrong, but only that something was not right.
The baby who had been using my insides for an *in
utero* jungle gym for eight months, the baby for
whom I had made balloon shades and wallpapered,
the baby I knew was probably going to be my last
was not growing. And no one could tell me why.

The last weeks of the pregnancy were weeks of
wondering, *Will I have this baby? Will it be okay? Will
I be okay if it isn't?* And there were the tests. Ultra-
sounds and stress tests. Non-stress tests and blood
tests. No answers, no clues, just a baby that wasn't
growing.

Winter was more than just a calendar occurrence
that year. The baby's due date was February 14—
Valentine's Day. January was a month of not knowing. A month of dark, brooding moments, with fears
held at bay and occasional tears.

My winter darkness ended that year on January 28. She was born, whole and healthy, but so small. Her head was no bigger than a tennis ball. And we named her Kari, drawing from the Greek word for grace, *charis*.

I know women miscarry. Babies are stillborn. And babies die. If I credit God with her birth, do I also then blame him for what the doctors termed "symmetrical growth retardation"? Answers to those questions I'll never know, but I do know Kari was a gift of grace. No one could explain it. We didn't earn her or deserve her. She was born. She was healthy. She was a gift of grace. And I thanked God—whether he was the cause or the cure—because I know he is present in moments of wonder.

 *Gifts of grace can seldom be understood or explained, only accepted with a grateful heart, a few blessed tears, and open arms.*

It will take a warmer heart than mine to hear a snow-covered gospel.[6]
—*Macrina Wiederkehr*

There was a time when faith came easily. When the touch of God in my life was new and his presence was as intimate as my own rhythmic breathing. I remember times when prayer was a spontaneous response to the fullness within, when my heart was full of promise and my faith was one of ready answers. Then something changed. I was confused, bewildered. I was doing all the same things, seeking in all the same ways, yet something within me had died. God had become distant, remote, and unreachable. I would read the saying on posters or cards, "When God seems distant, who moved?" and feel guilty—or angry—as if an invisible cosmic finger pointed at me accusingly.

Then I came across a line in a book by John Vannorsdall with which my heart resonated: "We heard so much about the presence of God that we were unprepared for the long absences of God."[7] The absences of God. There. The words were spoken. I was not the only one who had experienced the absences of God. The absence of God was through no lack of spiritual performance on my part, simply an ebb and flow of the spiritual life.

Theologians and thinkers through the centuries have written of the dark night of the soul, the spiritual wall, the wintry seasons of the heart. I have now come to understand that wintry spirituality is as true to the biblical tradition as the intimacy of the incarnation. I am no less faithful for acknowledging the questions without answers, the doubts that hover like low hanging clouds, and tears that obscure my view of a hidden God. For it is only in the winter of the heart, the season when all is seemingly dormant, that depth can take root, compassion is born, and honesty becomes a pillar of my faith. For if this God I worship is not a god who welcomes an honest seeker, how can he be worthy of my devotion?

I am no stranger to the winter of the heart. But I am in good company. Others have gone before me through the seasons of faith.

Hear my prayer, O LORD,
And give ear to my cry;
Do not be silent at my tears;
For I am a stranger with You.
—Psalm 39:12

All of life gives us the opportunity to experience God.

—*Marilyn Beckstrum*

*R*etract-o-legs. That's what we called my 18-month-old daughter's reaction to her first deep snowfall. Katy, my five-year-old, could hardly wait while the bundling process took place. At last, all the boots were on, the fingers were protected with mittens, the jackets were zipped, and hats were pulled on. Bundled up in a mishmash of clothing, Katy blasted out the door while her little sister, Kari, quietly watched.

Thinking she was simply a little hesitant, I carried her outside to experience this white wonder. I didn't need to worry about boots for her. Her feet never made contact with the snow. As I started to set her down, up came her legs, as if she had managed to physically pull them back into her body. Retract-o-legs! She would have nothing to do with that cold, uninviting, white stuff.

Her face was transparent: "Hey guys! What happened to solid ground? Give me some of that good old firm dead grass. Forget this weird stuff. I want our yard back!"

Not once during the entire winter would she let me set her down in the snow. No matter how I encouraged, suggested, or demonstrated, she was not to be convinced—not even by her sister who could usually talk her into anything. She was a skeptic, pure and simple. No winter play for her. She wanted what she knew, the tried and true.

I'm not really surprised. I'm that skeptic. I want to weigh the consequences of my choices before jumping in. I want evidence of security before putting my feet down.

When it comes to trusting God, we can easily have retract-o-faith. By pulling back and holding onto our anxieties and fears, we frequently miss the joy of the moment.

God, give me the faith to experience the unknowns, the unexpected, without pulling back in "retract-o-faith."

The LORD will open to you His good treasure, the heavens, to give the rain to your land in its season, and to bless all the work of your hand.

—Deuteronomy 28:12

*H*ere I sit. A rainy weekday morning. The dreariness is contagious. I know the rain is good for farmers and plants. But I'm not a farmer and unlike plants, the rain dampens my spirit, not my roots.

How do we muster any enthusiasm on days like today? Days of downcast spirits, a heavy heart, and responsibilities that feel overwhelming? Even the writers of the Old Testament occasionally needed reminders, so after years of oral tradition they finally wrote the words down that we now find in the Bible.

Today I need to hear this Old Testament reminder: "The LORD will open to you His good treasure." As I read these words, I wonder what treasure can be found in rainy days, dreary skies, and melancholy moods? The answer softly comes to me— reassurance. Reassurance that I'm not in this alone. Just as the fathers of my faith, I'm starting in the right place. I'm coming to a moment of quiet and seeking the presence of God. Only he can bring order to my confusion, encouragement to my work-weary world, and enthusiasm to my dreary heart. So God, this one's for you. This day and all that lays before me I put in your hands. The rain. The fatigue. The responsibilities. The part of me that feels stretched beyond my limits. This day I give to you, knowing your limits are infinite and your love is inexhaustible.

Lord, reframe my thinking as I go into this day, and let me learn from my tendency to overcommit myself. I give you this dreary day and my heavy heart—and ask that with the rain come showers of your grace . . . in my thinking, my working, my living.

And He was withdrawn from them . . .
and He knelt down and prayed.

—Luke 22:41

Christmas shopping was wearing thin. The little girl was about three years old, obviously tired and pushed beyond her limits. The line waiting at the register was long and moving slowly. Her mother's patience was stretched to the breaking point, and her voice was impatient. Standing behind them, I watched the scene unfold.

"Straighten up and be nice," the mother said as the three-year-old began to cry and whine.

"Mommy, I'm all out of nice," came the response.

I couldn't help but smile.

Haven't we all been there? All out of nice. Ready to go home, put on "comfy" clothes, and leave behind the hassles, the waiting, the stressful situations.

I think Jesus had times when he was "all out of nice." Luke, more so than any other writer of the gospels, records that Jesus withdrew. He got away from the crowds, the demands, the high-profile nature of his life. "He withdrew . . . and prayed."

These are good words for us to remember, whether we're "all out of nice" from Christmas shopping or from anything else. Failing to take time apart, and to go to the source, particularly during

highly demanding times, is setting us up for depletion, for finding ourselves "all out of nice."

*The times we think we don't have time to
pray are usually the times we most need
to.*

Your ears shall hear a word behind you,
   saying,
"This is the way, walk in it,"
Whenever you turn to the right hand
Or whenever you turn to the left.
                                    —*Isaiah 30:21*

*E*very year in late autumn the warning signs are posted. Then they are removed within six weeks. Late winter brings them out again. Neon orange, they're hard to miss. And the warning is succinct: Thin Ice.

When we first moved to Minnesota, we naively asked our realtor, "Do these lakes and rivers freeze over during the winter?"

"Oh, yes, most of them do," she replied professionally, somehow managing to keep a straight face.

Only months later did we realize what a comical question we had asked. "Do the lakes and rivers freeze over in Minnesota?" You bet they do. The ice can be twelve to twenty-four inches thick in southern Minnesota, and several feet thick further north. Minnesotans drive cars on the ice, set up warming huts for skating and fishing, and cross country skiing. Lakes and ponds become winter playgrounds.

But every year, despite the early and late season

warning signs, someone who is too eager to brave the ice early in the season becomes a tragic statistic. As a newcomer to Minnesota, I listened to news reports of heroic rescues or tragic endings to the inevitable consequences of thin ice and wondered, *How could anyone be so careless, so stupid?* Yet the answer is surprisingly simple. Ice is beguiling, deceptive. Thick enough to support a house or shingle thin, by appearance you can't tell the difference.

How easy and tempting it is to walk on thin ice. I do it all too often—financially, relationally, spiritually. Thin ice provides false security, but so do the things I look to for security: a bank balance of substance, a relationship that won't let me down, or seeking a safe haven from fears and anxieties.

Yet the source of surefooted movement is as near as a moment of prayer. A tentative intuition, a word softly whispered in the quiet of early morning meditation, a strength given in times of weakness—these are the safeguards to the thin ice around me if I only pay attention.

Thin ice is beguilingly deceptive. Am I walking on thin ice today?

Oh wind . . .
. . . O, wind,
If Winter comes,
Can Spring be far behind?
　　　　　　　　　—*Percy B. Shelley*

*S*omewhere between the lingering shadows of autumn days and the tulips and daffodils of early spring lies a siege of short days, long nights, and nasty weather. And despite knowing that this season, too, shall pass, I still succumb to the haunting spell of winter with those nagging feelings that it will always and forever be this way. Spring will never come. The skies will never clear. I will never be thin. And whatever difficult circumstances I'm facing now will never be resolved. Dark thoughts with circular repetition crowd out clear thinking just as dark skies dim the sun. Those nagging thoughts are my winter myth.

Sometimes I'm caught between what my heart is feeling and what my head is thinking. And the result is fatigue, restlessness, or depression. Knowing winter will not last forever does not make me feel any better, give me more energy, or even brighten my day, just as knowing my circumstances are not always and forever does not lessen my anxiety.

Connecting what I *know* to be true with the knot

in my stomach and the concerns of my heart is seldom within my power. But it *is* within God's power. Giving God my tomorrows, seeking his presence in this day disarms the winter darkness and frees me from the lure of the winter myth. Only God is always and forever—and he is trustworthy for my todays.

God, take my dark thoughts and bring your warming sun into my winter spirit. You know the concerns, the fears, the myths that cloud my world. Let me hear your gentle truth today that I may walk into my winter world wrapped in the cloak of your loving spirit.

> *When one has much to put into them, a day has a hundred pockets.*
> — *Friedrich Wilhelm Nietzsche*

I have a Dennis the Menace cartoon that has permanent residency on my desk during the winter months. With a grimacing frown, Mr. Wilson is shoveling deep, wet snow, while more snow is falling. Dennis is standing behind him saying, "Boy! Don't ya feel sorry for the folks who live down south?"

On any given day, the character I identify with in the cartoon changes. One day I'm clearly Mr. Wilson, begrudgingly shoveling yet another three inches of snow from our l-o-o-o-ong driveway. The next day I'm Dennis, loving every minute of winter's biting cold.

We all have a grimacing grump and an enthusiastic child within us. One resists what the other embraces. Wading my way through responsibilities, obligations, and necessities, the grump allows reality to narrow the boundaries of my world. But not today. Today I want to embrace the child within, be open to the surprises of the world around me, allow for moments of delight. I may even giggle. Or make a funny face in the car mirror on my way to somewhere very "adult." Maybe today I'll do something silly, or fun, or unplanned.

Maybe today I'll think of myself as Dennis the Menace and see if I can get into some harmless mischief.

I looked, blinked hard, then looked again, and before reason could stifle the impulse, my lips formed the name of one I loved who had died recently. Fighting to restrain embarrassed tears and swallowing hard to dispel the lump in my throat, I looked down realizing it couldn't be who I first thought. I then looked around sheepishly to see if anyone had seen me.

The experience was so real, so unsettling. For a brief moment, I was so *sure* of what I thought I saw, only to realize it couldn't be. If the reality of what we can see, hear, and touch in such tangible moments can cause us to question ourselves, how much more can issues of faith and feelings be subject to questions, second-guessing, and doubts?

As we near the holidays memories seem more poignant, expectations more intense, and secrets of the past scar the present. The very homecomings we look forward to can also bring mixed emotions and unexpected tears.

In times of mixed emotions, painful realizations, and hamstrung expectations, I long for certainty, for stability, for clarity. Yet perhaps it is in our times of doubt God finds a willing spirit. Perhaps our mixed emotions lead us to seek healing. Perhaps we are most receptive to God's leading when we aren't quite so confident of the answers.

Doubts, questioning, confusion lead us on journeys of discovery; when we willingly embrace the process, we come to know God in profoundly deeper ways on the other side.

> Indeed, the darkness shall not hide from
>   You,
> But the night shines as the day;
> The darkness and the light are both alike
>   to You.
>
> —Psalm 139:12

*H*ave you ever noticed how much harder it is to get out of bed in the early morning darkness of winter months compared to waking in the plentiful daylight of summer? An alarm clock is such an intrusion to the comfort of a cocoon of covers and a warm pillow. Yet the day begins—with or without early morning sun—and school, work, or responsibilities command my attention. Reluctantly I place my feet on the cold floor, grope for my well-worn houseshoes, and turn the lights on.

Except for a few diehard night owls, I know of few people who prefer the darkness of winter mornings to the bright light of summer sunshine streaming in through shutters and blinds of bedroom windows. Like moths dancing around lamplight or puppies stretched out in small patches of sunlit floor, we seek the welcoming warmth of light.

I can imagine the psalmist sitting on a dewy hillside among the quiet stirrings of sheep cloaked in early morning darkness. "Even the darkness is not dark to thee," the psalmist prays.

For centuries of biblical tradition, believers and seekers have prayed the Psalms. They are our first written collection of prayers of praise, thanksgiving, fear, anger, doubt—the full range of our human experience of a divine presence. In his book *A Cry of Absence* Martin Marty says, "Those who think that Praise the Lord defines the only Christian landscape, that the smile must be ever present and that, for the reborn, joy should always come easily . . . have to reject the classic text of Christian devotion."[9]

On mornings when I feel the darkness closing in, permeating my spirit and robbing me of the joy in living, I can turn to the Psalms as a living resource, a prayer journal, a source of comfort when I find myself yearning for the light.

God, even the darkness is as light with you. Bring your warming light into my chilly darkness today. Light my way that I may see clearly your gentle leading.

> *She has made the mundane the edge of glory.*
>
> *—Esther de Waal*

Scraps of fabric. Bits of this and that destined for the trash. Until placed in the gnarled, calloused hands of a woman whose face is lined with years of living. No longer are they mismatched scraps of this and that once the quilter works her magic and transforms remnants into a work of art, a source of warmth.

Her name is Esther and she's been quilting longer than I have lived. Her world reaches no further than the grocery store, the church, and occasional trips to the homes of her grown sons. Her home is simple and her face is uncluttered with makeup or mascara.

Yet when the quilting frame comes out, the marking pen goes to work, and her fingers fly with practiced ease between the fabric and a threaded needle, she becomes an artist.

I'm sure she doesn't see it that way. In her way of thinking, she's making something functional, something to meet a need. Yet to the outside observer, she's sewing bits of eternity, transforming ordinary calicos and muslin into something of beauty. Watching her work, I find myself thinking what a parable of God's love her quilting provides.

We are bits of this and that. With our lives often fragmented and torn, we feel like remnants. Yet this Master Quilter, this God of grace with whom nothing is wasted, pieces together the torn, the fragmented, and the remnants. In his hands, we are becoming beautiful, whole, and complete. The more fragmented the pieces of our lives are, the more intricate the divine design becomes. And in the end, who knows what warmth, what comfort, our lives will have offered to others. In the Quilter's hands nothing is wasted.

Lord, I give you the fragments and the pieces of my life, and trust the completion process to your divine design.

I have seen many of God's wonders;
Now I return to the concrete
   problems of life.
I shall search, and I shall find
Value in work, peace in my soul.
                   —Bula E. Legg

A story by Flannery O'Connor pictures an elderly couple who had lived in a little cabin in the Appalachians all their lives, sitting in their rocking chairs overlooking the mountains. The man says, "Well, Sarah, I see there's still some snow up there on the mountain."

In a little book called *Grace Notes and Other Fragments* Joseph Sittler writes,

> Now he knew there was snow on the mountain every year. She knew there was snow every year. So why does he have to say it? Because . . . to know that at times there is snow and at times there is not snow . . . was part of . . . an eternal rhythm which made their life together. In marriage you say the same things over and over, you inquire about the same people; and this is ho-hum in one way. . . . But it is breathtaking in another.[10]

Snow on the mountain. Mortgage payments to be mailed. Clothes at the drycleaners. Fragments of daily life. Sometimes we may feel we're only going through the motions, yet the very ho-hum nature of going through the motions is indicative of patterns of familiarity, patterns of commitment that give our lives structure.

Spirituality is no different. Our relationship to God is one of seasons, a rhythm of intimacy and distance, movement and stillness, doing and being. Prayer can become perfunctory. Service can feel obligatory. Rituals can become stale. Rather than welcoming the seasons of vitality and sameness as part of an inevitable rhythm of walking with God, we too easily panic, and wonder *what am I doing wrong?*

When wrestling with the undercurrents of spiritual ebbs and flows, we can count on the faithfulness of God and be reassured that our experience is as true to the spiritual life as breathing is to bodily life. God's presence in our lives and the transforming power of his spirit is not contingent on our ebbs and flows. When we feel as if we are only going through the motions with God, we can trust God to honor our faithfulness.

 *God, if you are trying to tell me something through this season of "snow on the mountain," could you make it a little more obvious? I'm wearying of going through the motions; I need to feel a fresh breeze stirring.*

Keep your eyes on the Prince of Peace.
—Henri J. M. Nouwen

*M*y daughters, at the ages of two and five, weren't bound by seasonal protocol. They hadn't yet realized that after January 1 the rest of the world put away their Christmas tapes and abandoned the well-worn carols for another year. On into January and well past Valentine's Day, they asked for the same tape—Amy Grant singing traditional, time-honored carols. As Amy Grant's velvety voice sang the lyrics I could repeat in a coma, my girls sang with abandon, off key, to their own interpretive melodies everywhere we went in our mini-van. We lived weeks past Epiphany traveling around town listening to Amy Grant's Christmas score.

I didn't have the heart to tell them we were probably the only family still cruising to "rocking around the Christmas tree, have a happy holiday," or "chestnuts roasting on an open fire." Driving the ballet carpool one day, I was sheepishly embarrassed when my other passengers looked a bit quizzical as they got into our van and Christmas carols were playing. I considered "losing" the tape. I suggested other tapes, but nothing worked. Amy was the artist of choice, and her Christmas tape was the only acceptable repertoire.

I gave up. Why not? Why have we pigeonholed those beautiful lyrics and moving melodies to one month of the year? We all want to take part of the Christmas spirit into the new year. Two little girls' love affair with a woman they know only through a voice kept Christmas alive in our family for months and I had to ask myself, *How many other experiences of the sacred, the holy, do I cut myself off from prematurely—merely because of calendar dates?*

 *Lord, let me break with seasonal protocol and savor the presence of the Christ child, the gift of grace unearned, no matter what the calendar date.*

For now we see in a mirror, dimly, but then face to face. Now I know in part, but then I shall know just as I also am known.

—1 Corinthians 13:12

Dim sun. I had never heard that phrase before moving to Minnesota. Partly cloudy. Partly sunny. Those phrases I was familiar with, but dim sun? Surprisingly, it is a phrase used regularly in upper midwest weather forecasts. And when dim sun occurs, no other phrase captures it quite so well. A gray, overcast sky with a faint white sphere visible through the clouds.

Nothing looks more wintry than overcast skies with dim sun peering through. A reminder that sunny days are possible, and a promise that the sun does still shine, but so far from the brilliance of crystal-clear, blue-sky days.

I wonder how much of our understanding of God and ourselves is like dim sun. We see a faint image, we have a promise of his presence, but our vision is so limited.

The biblical tradition is laced with people of faith who see God with limited vision. They encounter a presence obscured, but act on faith nonetheless, only to realize the divine initiative in unexpected moments of clarity. Moses and the burning bush. Jacob wrestling with the angel. Peter on the Mount of Transfiguration. The disciples on the road to Emmaus.

The divine initiative continues punctuating our days with moments of clarity. The aged, wrinkled face of a great grandmother whose eyes alight at my arrival. The gleeful greeting of a child flinging herself into my arms when we come together again at the end of a day. The lump in the throat when tender words are spoken to a wounded heart. These are moments we experience the divine initiative, moments when the dim sun burns through and we see clearly the face of Christ in one another.

"When the student is ready, the teacher appears," states an anonymous saying. Perhaps we see as much as we're ready to see; and our moments when the dim sun burns through are nothing we can orchestrate, but only experience with open hearts. Perhaps dim sun is for our own equilibrium. If we saw it all with the clarity of God's holiness, it would knock our socks off.

Lord, my understanding of many things is incomplete, my perspective is limited. I give my life to you, even when dim sun clouds my view. Open my eyes, my ears, my heart to your divine initiative.

*Anything worth doing is worth doing badly
on the way to doing it goodly.*

—*Jill Briscoe*

*H*e was forty, distinguished, successful, and lean. His thick black hair was giving way to gray. He was accustomed to being smooth, in control, and looking good. He knew how to excel . . . until he put on ice skates.

His normally athletic body, a powerful frame housing a gentle, loving scholar, instantaneously became an uncoordinated, comical combination of flailing arms, tangled feet, and spastic movements.

He gave skating five minutes, then retreated to the warming hut. Off came the skates and he watched from the sidelines as his five-year-old daughter flung herself across the ice, loving every slippery movement, giggling with every tumble.

The experience wasn't humorous for him; he couldn't laugh at his awkward, desperate scramble for balance—balance which wasn't possible on those thin blades and glazed surface.

"Anything worth doing is worth doing badly on the way to doing it goodly," says Jill Briscoe. What a wonderful twist of poor grammar, from a writer no less. Yet somewhere beyond the boundaries of childhood, we stop allowing ourselves the freedom to make fools of ourselves, to stretch beyond our comfort zones, to do something badly on the way to doing it goodly. At some point, performing well becomes more important than savoring the experience and being open to the new. Our fear of looking foolish can handicap our desires to change, to grow, to broaden our horizons.

"Unless you become like a little child. . . ." I don't think Jesus was limiting those words to entering the kingdom of heaven at some distant point in time. In many ways, the kingdom of heaven is now.

God is visible all around us, but only to
the man or woman who would see him.
—George MacDonald

*N*othing has had quite the same impact on me as standing on a winter beach, watching a fog bank roll in over the Gulf of Mexico. A wall of gray, it moved in so fast I actually watched it eating up the blue sky and the emerald water, rendering the horizon a whitewash of colorless gray. Closer and closer it moved, until finally, the gray enveloped the ground on which I stood. The waves at my feet only moments before were sparkling with the sun's reflection, now were a turbulent foam of brine.

Although I've spent years of my life watching the ebb and flow of Gulf tides, I've witnessed the fog bank phenomenon only once. One moment I was standing in the warmth of the South Texas sun; the next I was surrounded by a surreal world of minimal visibility. As I watched the wall of gray roll in I didn't move, knowing this was as rare as catching sight of a shooting star. Although eerie, the experience wasn't frightening. Rather, it was captivating—as if living inside a moment of magic—much like the transforming grace of God. At times God's grace is a presence so real that the moment is tangible. Then again, it is as ethereal as a fog bank recomposing an expanse of sea. But always present, always interrupting our ordinary lives with moments of wonder—if we only take the time to see.

Lord, open my eyes today to the moments of wonder you lay before me. Whether an unexpected tear or a much-needed laugh, open my eyes to the gift of life I have in this moment.

You need not cry very loud: he is nearer to us than we think.

—*Brother Lawrence*

*B*unnies and storytellers seem to go hand in hand. Although *The Velveteen Rabbit* is probably the most universally loved, another marriage between bunnies and the storyteller's pen is the story of Barrington Bunny.[11]

Barrington finds a baby field mouse stranded in a blizzard and covers him with his furry warmth throughout the storm. The next day the mother and father field mice are so caught up in the joy of finding their missing little one, they don't stop to consider the identity of the carcass of a dead bunny—and no one noticed the silent gray wolf who stood in the shadows watching over the dead bunny throughout the day and into the night.

How troubling the story of Barrington Bunny was to me when I first read it. I didn't want Barrington to die; I want happy endings and joyful reunions. Yet Barrington's story is our story. Loved ones die. Dreams are shattered. Things don't always work out the way we hope. How easy it is to think of God as the author of suffering, when in reality, he is our companion through it. When blinded by blizzards and withstanding winds of life, I take comfort in the image of a silent, gray wolf, knowing my fears well, and strengthening me with his presence to do what I have to do.

God, I don't need guarantees that my life won't be touched by suffering or heartache; I just need the strength to deal with the storms that come, knowing you are present and will see me through the darkness.

First keep the peace within yourself, then you can also bring peace to others.
—Thomas Kempis

We all know the feeling when wind, humidity, and hormones conspire to get the best of us. A bad hair day. No matter what we do our hair has a mind of its own, and we are anything but in harmony. I'm convinced that some days my hair is possessed, and my hair is just the beginning. Bad hair days always seem to be accompanied by an alarm clock that doesn't go off. A car that won't start. An umbrella left at home on a day of thunderstorms. A "to do" list that clones itself overnight.

Once a bad hair day takes hold, is there any antidote? Is there any way to take ownership of my spirit again and let go of the silent snarls within?

I know of only two antidotes—humor and kindness. Not directed at others, but rather humor and kindness aimed at myself. After all, even Jesus withdrew for time to himself. We can only give to others what we first give to ourselves. One woman says, "Give from your extra, not your essence."

Bad hair days are usually an indicator that something is out of whack, tensions are high, and my inner reservoir is depleted. I need to slow down, back up, and place my mood, my day, my challenges, and my life in God's care—and leave them there. After giving myself permission to withdraw momentarily from the demands, I need to ask myself, *What do I need today? Laughter or kindness? Rest or focus? Have I been taking myself—and my hair—too seriously?*

God, loosen the hold on me created by bad hair days, and free me to listen to my heart's desires. Free me to experience your love in small acts of kindness. Even Jesus needed time apart, time to replenish.

*S*he is in the winter of her life. She now has more gray hair than dark. Her once deep, brown eyes are now slightly cloudy, as if she's looking at her world through an early morning mist. Her day is punctuated by regular maintenance medications and she looks back on more years than she has left to anticipate.

And she grieves the chill of an estranged relationship with one of her children. Blaming herself, she struggles to let go of the "if onlys" and longs for the warmth of reconciliation. She lives with the dull ache of unspoken anger and the sting of love turned dutiful.

Winter's cold is not always cozy and the winter years are not always golden. Yet we each, in our own ways, do the best we can for those we love. Our love is always human, always short of perfection. We, too, will be inadequate stewards of our children's childhoods, incapable of meeting the needs of those we would wish to spare from all of life's hurts and disappointments.

Although I can't offer healing to one who lives in the winter years or bears a wintry heart, I can offer hope. The God of spring's new life, of summer's joy, and of autumn's fullness, is also the God of winter's chill. Although we never know what lies buried beneath the frozen stillness, we can trust that surely, surely, after winter comes the spring.

Surely, surely, after winter comes the spring.

Never be in a hurry; do everything quietly and in a calm spirit. Do not lose your inward peace for anything whatsoever, even if your whole world seems upset. Commend all to God, and then lie still and be at rest in His bosom.

—St. Francis de Sales

Why is it when the world around me is frozen in silent stillness, I can be so frenetic within? Commitments, responsibilities, obligations, engagements, deadlines all too quickly clutter my calendar.

I walk outside and the air is cold, clear, fresh. The only movement of the wind is the rhythmic sound of my own breathing. Yet within I feel like a washing machine stuck on the spin cycle. Despite my best intentions, I can't seem to slow down.

In God alone will I find my calm, my stillness. And it is only when I commend all to him that I find the knots in my stomach untied, the tension in my shoulders released, and the person within freed from the clamor of voices and demands.

Lord, I feel the press of too many things commanding my attention. I unrealistically try to do it all at once. Slow me down. Quiet the pressures and anxieties and bring my inner spinning to a stop as you lead me through the demands and order my priorities.

 *God, when I feel like a washing machine stuck on spin, help me bring my spinning to a halt.*

*Cleaning your house while your kids are
still growing is like shoveling the walk
before it's stopped snowing.*

—*Phyllis Diller*

A woman's life is one of accepting the incomplete.

A trip to the grocery store today does not free me from the need to do it again next week. Clothes are washed, dried, folded, and neatly placed in drawers only to be pulled out in haste, worn, and thrown in the hamper again. Dirty dishes must find ways to clone themselves. We surely don't go through *that* many glasses!

Within the frustration of the seemingly unending round-robins of a woman's life there is a reminder of powerful significance. We are part of the rhythm of life. Once there are no more groceries to buy, clothes to launder, or dishes to wash, life has, in some sense, ceased.

Our challenge is to keep our frustration with the incomplete balanced with our yearning for a sense of accomplishment. We live in a tug-of-war of tensions much like savoring a novel that we don't want to end, while eagerly devouring the conclusion anyway. Once we've read the final chapter, the book is finished. Although we can reread the story, we can never read it again with the same sense of wonder, anticipation, or discovery.

The Practice of the Presence of God, a contemplative classic by Brother Lawrence, is a collection of conversations and letters by a humble man who served in a monastery in the kitchen. Brother Lawrence was described as having a great aversion to kitchen duty. Not one to take great pleasure from working in the kitchen, Brother Lawrence and I are kindred souls! Nonetheless, he approached his tasks with the prayer, "Lord, I cannot do this unless Thou enablest me."

What a wonderful perspective I can learn from a Carmelite monk who lived three hundred years ago and enjoyed doing dishes no more than I. He knew the frustration in tasks of repetition, yet he gave himself to his tasks while seeking the presence of God.

 *Lord, I cannot do this unless you enable me. In the middle of unending tasks and frustrating moments, give me a silent gratitude for the fullness of this season of my life.*

Welcome an inbreaking of the sacred.

I was going to be unbelievably productive. Get up early. Cup of coffee sitting on my desk by 7:00. Computer on and the project underway.

She had other ideas.

She is the consummate putter-bug. A mite-sized introvert, she can frequently entertain herself for hours with stuffed bunnies, small plastic horses lined up in rows, or coloring crayons and computer paper pulled out of our recycling box.

But this morning, she had other ideas.

At age three, her opinions are definitive; her preferences not the least wishy-washy. She knows exactly what she wants, when she wants it, and who is to give it. And she has an effectively persuasive means of getting what she wants—big blue eyes that could melt the frozen Klondike.

This morning my productivity was not on her agenda. This morning she wanted to be in my lap, not sitting in my office on the floor entertaining herself as is her usual custom. No. Right in my lap, seated in front of my computer blocking my fingers from the keyboard, she was content.

Kids have a way of knowing what their needs are and getting them met with none of the usual adult subtleties. She perched herself in my lap for the better part of an hour. And I let her. She began scribbling with a pen, as I encircled her with my arms, reached for the keyboard, and began working with my nose tickled by a tangle of curls. We both got what we needed.

And into my cold, productive winter morning, came a touch of spring.

Interruptions can bring aggravations—or a touch of unexpected grace.

> *We are healed of suffering only by*
> *experiencing it to the full.*
>
> —*Marcel Proust*

*A*nyone who's played in the snow as a child knows the pain of cold fingers and toes from remaining outside too long. Our circulation reminds us that human anatomy is not designed to accommodate prolonged exposure to frigid temperatures, as the burning, stinging sensation bring tears and vows of never doing that again.

No matter what our age or the source of our suffering, pain gets our attention. We can deny or medicate it, ignore or tolerate it, but pain will have the last say. Whether emotional or physical, distancing ourselves from pain buys time, but not solutions.

In an essay from *The Clown in the Belfry,* Frederick Buechner writes, "We are never more alive to life than when it hurts—never more aware both of our own powerlessness to save ourselves and of at least the possibility of a power beyond ourselves to save us and heal us if we can only open ourselves to it."[12]

Opening ourselves to pain is born of leaning into our emotions, our circumstances, our hurts, and our hopes, and thereby walking through our pain to the healing on the other side. If our singular goal is to simply eradicate pain, we miss the saving grace to be found within. Pain, particularly emotional pain, is often the seedbed of sanctified discontent, providing the inner momentum to move us out of ruts, damaging relationships, and destructive situations. Pain is always a catalyst for action.

There is no pain so dark and fearsome that God cannot be found within it.

*Everybody thinks of changing humanity
and nobody thinks of changing himself.*
—*Leo Tolstoy*

*S*nowbirds. That's what we always called them.
They were folks from the north who sought the
milder temperatures of the sunbelt in the harshest
months of winter. Some locals resented their annual
migratory invasion, while others welcomed their
business. But almost everybody considered them
different. One of "them," not one of "us."

Distinctions. Differences. Categories.

How tempting is the universal tendency to cate-
gorize people we meet. We place them safely in little
boxes in our minds labeled "familiar" or "unfamil-
iar" while denying our prejudices. Blue-collar or
white-collar; white or black; educated or underpriv-
ileged. Labels become boxes in our minds into
which we can admit or reject the people we encounter from day to day.

But differences aside, we really are more alike
than different. And we never know through whom
God may want to speak to us, get our attention, or
touch our hearts.

The person who most aggravates me is quite possibly a reflection of my own shadow side, that part
of me that I most dislike, struggle with, or find

embarrassing. Before too quickly casting judgment on another, perhaps I need to ask God to help me turn the spotlight back on myself. Perhaps I could begin by praying for the person I find it difficult to deal with, and in doing so, I may be surprised by who experiences the greatest change in attitude— it just might be me.

Lord, let me see each individual who walks into my world today as a person created by you. Open my eyes to the labels and hidden prejudices that cloud my thinking.

Keep your heart with all diligence,
For out of it spring the issues of life.
—Proverbs 4:23

*W*atching the evening weather reports, I whimsically think, *Wouldn't it be great if we had internal radar?* Simply turn on an internal monitoring device, and locate the exact source, velocity, intensity of the storms of life. With internal radar we wouldn't be blindsided by unexpected events; storms of conflict could be tracked as they were developing; fronts bringing conditions of reduced visibility could at least be anticipated. Theoretically.

Unfortunately, even radar is inconclusive and weather forecasters are notoriously inaccurate. We just can't get around the fact that life is wonderfully, excruciatingly unpredictable, and this is especially true in matters of the heart.

"The heart knows and demands a listening to its confusion,"[13] writes Martin Marty. Yet tending to matters of the heart takes time, patience, trust— and it's not nearly as clinical as reading a radar report. But the rewards are infinitely fuller. For it is only in "keeping our hearts with all diligence" that we deepen in wisdom, grow in compassion, and live fully.

Life is not meant to be lived clinically. Life is

meant to be experienced knowing we've got a shelter through the storms—a living God at the heart of our faith.

God, I don't have radar; I only have you. As I bring before you the matters of my heart, give me reassurance that I can weather any storm surrounded by your love.

We must know where to doubt, where to feel certain, where to submit.

—*Blaise Pascal*

*S*itting on my bookshelf is a book published several years ago called *The Myth of Certainty*. The title alone catches my eye and speaks to me with a ring of truth. How I long for a world of black and white, good and bad, yes and no; a world of clear-cut distinctions and effortless decisions because the good and bad can be easily identified. No blurring rationalizations. No complicating considerations.

But clear-cut distinctions and effortless choices aren't true to my experience of life. Between black and white are shades of gray. Between good and bad are confusing questions. Between yes and no is a strong maybe.

The fact of the matter is, no matter how black and white and absolute some defenders of the faith portray the Gospel, I simply can't buy that line. My experience and the experience of people of faith throughout the centuries, is one of a God who meets us *in* the questions, who honors our seeking, and who created us to be intelligent beings. When it comes to faith, if we're looking for proof and certainty, we won't find it.

Living at the heart of faith is living with uncertainty, trusting in the unseen. Jesus said, "Blessed are those who have not seen and yet have believed" (John 20:29). Somewhere along the way, we have to leap the chasm between that which we know absolutely and that which calls us from within. Yet even in our uncertainty, we walk in the presence of the holy.

God is far more interested in our honesty than our piety. We have only to offer him a willing heart and truthful spirit and he'll take it from there, meeting us in the chasm as we make the leap.

God, you know what decisions I'm facing, the times I long for clarity and certainty, the struggle to know right from wrong in choices I must make. I want to do the right thing, yet any decision I make involves risk. Lord, I put my decisions, my choices, my uncertainty in your hands. May I be encircled by your grace, knowing you will give me as much clarity as I need for this day.

I will lift up my eyes . . .

—*Psalm 121:1*

Two ballerinas live in our household. Don't misunderstand—these are not classically trained ballerinas. These are half-pint, preschool dancers who careen through the house with abandon, spinning and turning to the music in their heads, only to fall when dizziness overtakes their precarious balance.

When television coverage of the Winter Olympics brought visions of twirling, whirling ice skaters into our home, we had two diminutive skaters in our living room. Spin after spin catapulted them into tangled heaps of arms and legs on the floor. Finally, my five year old asked in exasperation, "Mommy, how do they spin so fast?"

I tried to explain a technique learned many years ago when I was the ballerina-to-be—the technique of spotting. Start by focusing your sight on a fixed spot and with each rapid turn of the head, return your gaze to the same place. No dramatic improvement resulted from my little ballerina's initial efforts as she began trying this technique. Spotting does not come naturally at any age; she and her sister continued to look like they were playing a musical game of Twister, ending in the same heap on the floor. But slowly, ever so slowly, spotting took effect. Her turns were more controlled, she retained her balance, and before long she was trying to explain spotting to her little sister.

Spotting takes practice, but it works. And it's no different for grown-ups. On what do we set our sights? Are we spotting on career moves, relationships, things? What occupies our minds as we wake in the morning or creeps in unsolicited to our thoughts as we close our eyes at the end of the day? Our uninvited thoughts and recurring worries are probably a good indicator of what we're using to spot.

The psalmist wrote, "I will lift up my eyes . . . ." He knew about spotting, even if he didn't call it that. He knew where to set his sights. Only one thing is worthy of our practiced focus, and only one thing will enable us to maintain our balance. When my head is spinning and my world is turning too fast, I can spot on one whose power is greater than mine, one who never loses his balance.

 *Children aren't afraid to practice something awkward and new to accomplish a goal or perfect a skill. I need to take note; some things still require practice.*

How poor are they that have not patience!
What wound did ever heal but by degrees?
—*William Shakespeare*

Despite knowing cognitively that colds run their course, chicken pox is not terminal, and the flu is not usually permanent, I've often thought, *I'll have to die to get better.* Weeks go by in a blur of Kleenex and sinus headaches; one medication leaving me feeling semi-comatose, another giving me a jittery buzz.

The promises of relief from makers of cold and flu remedies always fall short of my hopes and expectations. I don't want minimal relief—I want immediate absolution!

Coughs and sneezes, sore throats and ear infections, fever and aches . . . ah, the many ways our bodies have of stopping us in our tracks. But we don't stop. We think we can't because we have too many things to do. So we medicate our aches and pains while going through the motions of responsibilities that won't wait.

Or will they? Schedules can be rearranged. Responsibilities can be shifted. And yes, some things can wait.

When we feel like our bodies have turned against us, we need to listen to the signals. The lives of those around us will not be permanently impaired if we stop, rest, and indulge in a little extra tender loving care.

The Apostle Paul wrote, "Do you not know that you are the temple of God and that the Spirit of God dwells in you?" (1 Corinthians 3:16). I am a temple of God? Do I take better care of those I love, or even my car or my house, than I do of myself?

Maybe I better rethink this. Maybe the next time I find myself an unwilling participant in winter's cold and flu season, I'll take the phone off the hook, stock up on a few paperback novels, and crawl back under the covers. It could just be that this temple is needing to be closed temporarily for repairs and renovation.

I am not indispensable, even if I find that hard to believe. When my body seems to be turning against me, maybe God is trying to get my attention.

> *You are My beloved Son; in You I am well pleased.*
>
> —*Luke 3:22*

*C*abin fever is a *very* real phenomenon when winters are long, temperatures are forbidding, and windchills are in the single digits. We often go to the area shopping malls just to get out of the house for a while, let our girls run off some pent-up energy, and give ourselves a break.

Recently I sat drinking a cup of coffee, watching my five-year-old daughter as she watched her own reflection in a store display window. Absorbed in her own pretend world, she sang, posed, and performed for her own entertainment—completely delighted with herself. Unaware that I was watching her, she continued her personal performance for some time.

I sat wondering, *When I see myself in a mirror, am I ever that pleased with what I see? Do I enjoy my own company as much as she is?*

Not too often, I had to admit. Moments of carefree, nonproductive daydreaming are not readily allowed in my grown-up, adult world. Self-appraisals for most women I know focus on too fat, too thin, too busy, or too tired. Moments of reflection and evaluation center on what we *haven't* done, what we *need* to do, or what we *plan* to do. We rarely give ourselves the opportunity to simply enjoy our own company.

But God told Jesus at the moment of his baptism, before he had done anything, "You are My beloved." Before Jesus accomplished anything, before he healed anyone, before he had a following, God's love was assured and was freely given as a gift.

Just as Jesus is God's son, so am I a child of God. John, the most poetic of the gospel writers, boldly proclaims, "Behold what manner of love the Father has bestowed on us, that we should be called children of God!" (1 John 3:1)

In God's eyes, we are the five-year-old dancing before the mirror of Christ's reflection. We are absolutely, completely, unconditionally loved and he is delighted with our performance—*before we've accomplished anything.* If God freely gives me his complete acceptance, can I do any less for myself?

Behold what manner of love the Father has bestowed upon us.

There is no event so commonplace but that God is present within it, always hiddenly, always leaving you room to recognize him or not to recognize him.[14]

—*Frederick Buechner*

It comes ever so softly. If you're busy or preoccupied, you can easily miss it. Quietly, it breaks into the world of manicured lawns and busy streets, of high-rise office buildings and inner city slums. Ghettos and suburbs alike are painted by its magic, a whitewash that softens the harsh city skylines and brings visible poetry to farmers' fields. The first snowfall of winter enters our lives.

No matter how many times I've experienced the soft intrusion of the first snowfall of the season, I'm always enchanted by its coming.

Rationally I know this is the first of many. I know the shoveling, the bundling, the hassles of winter are on their way. But those realities don't mar the incredible beauty of frosted flakes gently rearranging the view out my window with a simple wash of white.

"There is no event so commonplace but that God is present within it, always hiddenly, always leaving you room to recognize him or not to recognize him," writes Frederick Buechner.

No event so commonplace. A hidden God. A presence that steals into our lives like the season's first snowfall. So unlike the momentous, the pivotal, the turning points of our lives: receiving the diploma on graduation day, walking down the aisle toward the face of one we hope to grow old with at our wedding, pain giving way to joy in childbirth, the sudden tears as we are told a loved one didn't survive the surgery. Those are the momentous, the memorable, the transparent events that take us out of the ordinary. Those are the moments so few in each of our lives we can count them on one hand. If God only made his presence known in the momentous, how barren our lives would be of grace-filled windows to the sacred.

Instead, there are snowfalls and rain showers, waking and sleeping, as we live a succession of ordinary days. Into our ordinary world we are given this hidden God, one who comes to us as a baby born amid hay and barnyard smells to a nondescript couple on an ordinary night. Into the ordinary, came the extraordinary. The birth of a savior. And our lives will never be the same.

Ordinary moments. Extraordinary grace. Lord, let me see beyond this day to the precious gift of life I've been given.

God raises the level of the impossible.
—*Corrie ten Boom*

In the rugged desolation of the Sinai Desert is a scrubby little tree referred to in the Bible as the acacia tree. Dwarfed by the mountainous, barren rock formations jutting out across the arid land, acacia trees look like diminutive scrub brushes littering the landscape. How anything grows in the lifeless, rocky, windswept expanse of the Sinai is something of a miracle, yet here this tenacious tree makes its home—and it is found nowhere else.

This scrubby tree grows to be six to eighteen feet tall, yet beneath the rocky soil where no one can see, is a tap root extending to a depth of sixty to seventy feet. And this ugly little tree that grows where nothing else can, blooms after six months of drought. What a reversal of horticultural norms!

Where nothing else survives, one determined species has adapted itself to the harshest of conditions. Where no one can see, a tap root somehow manages to push its way through the rock to find a water source. When most everything else requires water, light, and favorable soil conditions, one little tree blooms when all the odds are against it.

When the winters of my life seem too much to bear and my soul longs for an end to the droughts, in whatever form they come, the acacia tree is something of a rainbow; a promise that with God nothing is impossible and I *will* survive. Like the acacia trees of the Sinai, I will bloom again even when the odds are against me.

God, I will extend my tap root ever further into your presence, knowing you will never fail me.

> *Therefore do not cast away your confidence, which has great reward. For you have need of endurance, so that after you have done the will of God, you may receive the promise.*
>
> —*Hebrews 10:35–36*

To say winters are long in Minnesota is to say that the sun rises in the east and sets in the west. Long winters are a fact, a non-negotiable, a given. Winter days sometimes feel as if the Ice Queen from the *Chronicles of Narnia* has unleased her frozen spell and the world is captive to her icy, unyielding reign.

Yet as spring nears, the snow begins to recede ever so gradually, almost imperceptibly. Slowly, jackets grabbed from the closet are lighter in weight, gloves are no longer necessary, hats are left indoors. The ground begins to be visible beneath the frozen snow. Signs of winter's demise do eventually appear.

Still, for those longing for the sun's warmth and spring's vivid greens, the changes are painfully slow in coming.

Our lives can sometimes feel as if nothing is happening. We wake, get dressed, go to work, and take care of responsibilities. We fix meals, pick up dry cleaning, and pay bills. Life is so *daily*. Trying to measure the depth of my relationship with God or the growth in my life is like trying to watch the snow melt—an unfulfilling exercise in futility.

Monitoring our spiritual or personal growth isn't up to us. This process, this daily living our faith, is as gradual (and as wonderful) as spring emerging. And like spring, the results aren't up to us. Our job is to be willing to let God be God, and to trust him with the results.

God, sometimes I feel so impatient. I want prayers answered now. I want to see changes in myself and changes in the ones I love. Yet change comes so slowly. When my concerns, my fears, my worries feel like a Minnesota snow pack refusing to melt, let me feel the warmth of your Son.

NOTES

1. Frederick Buechner, *Telling Secrets* (San Francisco: Harper San Francisco, 1973), p. 33.

2. Richard Foster, *Celebration of Discipline* (San Francisco: Harper San Francisco, 1988), p. 27.

3. Frederick Buechner, *Telling Secrets* (San Francisco: Harper San Francisco, 1991), p. 56.

4. Quoted in Reuben P. Job and Norman Shawchuck, *A Guide to Prayer for All God's People* (Nashville: Upper Room Books, 1990), p. 33.

5. Debra K. Klingsporn, "Dancing Leaves," 1993.

6. Macrina Wiederkeher, O.S.B., "Prayer to a Winter God," *Seasons of Your Heart* (San Francisco: Harper, 1991), p. 150.

7. John Vannorsdall, *Dimly Burning Wicks* (Minneapolis: Fortress Press, 1982), p. 11.

8. Frederick Buechner, *Alphabet of Grace* (San Francisco: Harper & Row, 1978), pp. 46–47.

9. Martin Marty, *A Cry of Absence* (San Francisco: Harper & Row, 1983), pp. 39–40.

10. Joseph Sitler, *Grace Notes and Other Fragments,* edited by Robert M. Herhold & Linda Marie Delloff (Philadelphia: Fortress Press, 1981), pp. 39–40.

11. Martin Bell, *The Way of the Wolf: The Gospel in New Images* (New York: Seabury Press, 1968), pp. 11–18.

12. Frederick Buechner, *The Clown in the Belfry* (San Francisco: Harper San Francisco, 1992), pp. 98–99.

13. Martin Marty, *A Cry of Absence* (San Francisco: Harper & Row, 1983), p. 55.

14. Frederick Buechner, *Now and Then* (San Francisco: Harper & Row, 1983), p. 87.

SPRING

a time to grow

When April with its gentle showers has
pierced the March drought to the root and
bathed every plant in the moisture . . .
when . . . small birds sing melodiously, so
touched in their hearts by nature that they
sleep all night with open eyes—then folks
long to go on pilgrimages.
—Geoffrey Chaucer

*W*inter's over. (Well, almost.) Sun's out (when it's not pouring rain). Air is warmer. Grass is turning green. Birds are getting busy. And I feel the urge to get busy too—to build something, grow something, clean something, make something, or just to get outside and move.

This stirring, no doubt, is biological, the result of being cooped up for too long. It's partially a primitive physiological response to longer days and more sunlight. But I think it's also a divine nudge—an impulse from my Creator to be about the business I was put on earth for.

And there's the rub, because I'm not always certain what that business is! Spring has given me the gift of renewed energy and a spurt of new hope, but I'm not clear what to do next. Maybe that's why my gardens often get planned but not plowed, my exercise programs don't last, my spring cleaning gets interrupted and goes unfinished.

Maybe before I fling open the door and run out-side, I need to spend some time inside . . . inside me. Before I get busy with whatever projects offer themselves, maybe I need to go on an inner pilgrim-age, to spend some time in journaling and prayer, to meditate on purpose and direction. I need to pray . . .

My God, you gave me this restlessness, this urge to get busy. Grant me the purpose to know what I need to do with it and the courage and commitment to follow through even when this surge of energy ebbs.

Love lives again, that with the dead has
*   been:*
Love is come again like wheat that
*   springeth green.*
                    —*John Macleod Campbell Crum*

*T*here's something about pain that just freezes a person up. When we've been hurt, when we've lost something or somebody we loved, we tend to tighten up, to shut down emotionally.

And this is not necessarily bad. Human protective mechanisms exist for a purpose. Psychologists tell us that depression is a normal and necessary response to loss; it's the body's way of slowing life down so that thoughts and feelings have time to adjust.

Just as winter allows the earth time to rest and prepare for new growth, emotional withdrawal can buy time for a wounded self to heal. But we can't stay frozen forever. We have to let ourselves thaw out.

A spring thaw can be gradual and gentle, the slow unfolding of a blossoming soul. Or it can be sudden and violent, like ice floes snapping and spring thunderstorms roaring. But with the thaw, sudden or gentle, comes release and the promise of greener days ahead.

 I need emotional defenses. But eventually I also need the grace and courage to let them go.

> *They considered keeping the soil constantly stirred about the roots of growing things the secret of success. . . . The process was called "tickling." "Tickle up old Mother Earth and make her bear!" they would shout to each other across the plots.*
> —Flora Thompson

I'm no gardener. My thumb has not a tinge of green. In fact, I routinely murder the plants my daughter brings home from school; those hopeful little sprouts in their egg-carton planters just don't have a chance. The idea of grubbing around outside in the dirt brings to my mind not romantic, earthy images but hot, itchy, sweaty ones. As a city girl raised by city folks, I'm pretty vague about what one even does with a hoe.

But while I've basically come to terms with being horticulturally challenged, I wonder if I'm missing one of the key messages of spring.

I've always seen springtime as play time, a time to leave cabin-fever winter behind and to run in the wildflowers. Spring fever always sets up a tug of war between revelry and responsibility. But to a gardener, spring is a time for action and for investment, a time to get started on the work that will bring a summer bounty. And the gardener gets to play at the same time—to dig in the dirt and enjoy the sunshine and look forward to the future.

I also envy gardeners' clear connection between their work and its outcome. Too often I drive to the store and then go to the track to walk. Too often I neglect my family so I can work to support them. Too often I sit at my desk to do my work but never meet the people it affects. But in gardening the connection between work and purpose is clear: you break the soil, you pull the weeds, you harvest the tomatoes or the zinnias. I find that refreshing . . . and instructive.

Dear God, teach me the secret of integrating work and play and purpose— and show me how to invest it all for the purpose of growth.

He has put eternity in their hearts, except
that no one can find out the work that God
does from beginning to end.

—*Ecclesiastes 3:11*

*I*n Texas, where I grew up, spring starts early—daffodils on Valentine's day, bright fields of bluebonnets in March, irises before April, roses before May. So I was fascinated when I first visited New England in June to see gardens full of irises and to hear that they had just finished with the daffodils. Back in Texas, lawns were already browning, and nature was already hunkering down under a hot summer sun!

That was the first time I really understood that not everybody's springtime happens at the same time. And that's not just true of the weather; that's the way people grow.

Most of us these days know about the various stages of human development. We expect to go through periods of separation and rebellion, growth and productivity, confusion and searching, certainty and contentment. But although it's helpful to know what to expect about the seasons of our lives, I think it can be dangerous to get too specific.

Every person is unique, with an individual set of body rhythms, past experiences, present circumstances. Individual responses and decisions shape the direction of our lives. Each of us experiences the seasons of life a little differently. And if we forget that, we easily fall into the trap of either comparing ourselves to others or judging them. Perhaps we can even bring on certain crises by anticipating them—as if it's "time" for an adolescent to rebel or a middle-aged executive to feel unfulfilled.

There's nothing wrong with being prepared for life's predictable crises. But we're not in charge of life's timetable. Springtime doesn't come at the same time for everyone—and that's true of summer, fall, and winter as well.

It's not our job to map out our lives—or anybody else's. It is our job to try to steer through each season with grace and integrity.

But I'm not dead yet . . .
— *British humorist*

If you've never lived with small children or received a balloon bouquet, you may not be aware that helium balloons have a half-life. They come home from birthday parties and other celebrations all plump and hopeful, bobbing energetically at the end of their strings. A few days later they're at half-mast—not buoyant but not yet deflated. If they're made of Mylar, like the ones my husband received for his birthday, they can go on indefinitely.

So after a couple of dozen birthdays, I've finally come to terms with the necessity of balloon murder. It's hard, even painful, to plunge scissors or a needle into one of those bright bubbles. But if I didn't take matters in hand, our lives would be continually haunted by the ghosts of birthdays past.

And this skill of balloon murder has not been a bad one for me to learn because I'm one of those people who have trouble letting go of a good thing. I resist throwing things away, ending involvements, saying *enough*. At times I've held on to people and places and relationships and jobs long after they stopped having a legitimate place in my life. Even though I know I need to clear the ground before anything new can grow, I often cling tenaciously to the status quo.

Not everybody has this particular problem. Some people seem to have a special knack for saying "the end." These people may even need to learn to be less ruthless and more patient. But I believe I'm put on this earth to learn what *I* have to learn—and in my case balloon murder is a helpful lesson.

 Lord, you go on forever, but not everything in my life has to! Grant me the wisdom to know when my "balloons" have seen their day. And remind me that if I stick with you, balloons will never be in short supply.

*Now to Him who is able to do exceedingly
abundantly above all that we ask or
think . . . to Him be glory.*
—*Ephesians 3:20–21*

Magazine articles and pop psychology books are always cautioning me about my expectations. Apparently many of my problems (and everybody else's problems) result from unrealistic, unexamined expectations.

Do I expect to be rescued by Prince Charming? I'd better think again.

Do I expect approval for what I do and what I am? I'd better find another source of self-esteem.

Do I expect people to read my mind? I'd better learn to communicate my wants and needs.

Do I expect life to be fair or even happy? I'd better get real!

And all this is helpful to a point. But after awhile I start wondering exactly what I *can* expect. Something deep within me rebels at the cynicism of the apparent message: "Expect nothing; that way you won't be disappointed."

So what *can* I reasonably expect from my life and my relationships? As far as I can tell, these are the basics:

- In this world, I can expect to have problems—sickness, rejection, tragedy, interrupted plans.
- I can expect God to be with me through it all. I can count on God's comfort and God's strength if I can remember to keep turning to him.
- I can expect that eventually, over the long term, things will work out for the best. Not necessarily the way I planned. Not necessarily in ways I can see at the time. Not necessarily even in my lifetime. But I can reasonably expect that God will remain in charge and will continue to be good and loving.
- I can expect to be surprised with even more than I ever thought to expect—more than I could ever ask for or think about—if I keep myself focused on God's purposes.

Exactly how this all works is a mystery— I can't expect to understand it all. But I can trust you, Lord, to be with me as I learn to adjust my expectations.

> *Loneliness is the secret we keep from*
> *ourselves as well as from others.*
> —Elizabeth O'Connor

The question was *In what social circles or times of your life have you felt "out of it"—like a stranger in a strange land?*

And the answer from almost everyone in the room was *I feel that way right now.*

"Since I graduated from college, I've had trouble finding women friends my age."

"I've lived in this town three years, and I don't have a single friend I can call on the spur of the moment and go out with."

"We rent in an upper-middle-class neighborhood, but we just don't have the money or time to live like our neighbors."

"I can't relate to the people I work with, and after work and dinner and time with my family, there's no time left to meet anybody else."

These were all normal, well-adjusted, productive people. All had families, jobs, activities. And all were surprised to realize just how painfully isolated and out of place they felt—at least part of the time!

Loneliness is epidemic in our cities and towns, in our workplaces, and in our churches and PTAs. It's partly because we move around so much, partly because we're so busy, partly because we're wary of strangers. Partly because it's human nature to drift into isolation unless we take specific steps to stop the drift.

I don't have the answers to this problem. I'm lonely too. But that night, in a circle of strangers, I saw connections being made. We admitted our loneliness to each other and to ourselves, and we sowed seeds of friendship and community. It was a good first step.

Lord, help me to tell the secret of my loneliness and then to look beyond it to the loneliness of others. Help me keep in mind that relationships aren't a luxury—and help me to make time in my life for the development and nurture of friendships.

Those who sow in tears shall reap in joy.
—Psalm 126:5

A man on our street when I was growing up took all the grass out of his front yard and replaced it with gravel. He had a heart condition and wasn't supposed to do yard work. I can understand that. Besides, rock gardens look great.

But the strange thing was that this man insisted on *green* gravel. And he was the crankiest neighbor of all about keeping kids off his "lawn." Although he skipped the work of sodding and fertilizing and mowing, it seemed he still wanted to convince himself and others that he was growing grass. Of course, he wasn't fooling anybody. And he still had to do the work of defending his turf.

I think I sometimes do something similar with my own growth. I've done a lot of reading about spiritual growth and emotional healing. I'm familiar with what it means to be healthy. But much of the time, instead of investing in self-examination and real change, I put out some green gravel and *act* as though I've changed. Instead of working through my anger, I act mature. Instead of revealing my inner self to others, I act honest. Instead of tackling my selfishness and self-absorption, I act unselfish. Instead of "listening to my life" (to borrow Frederick Buechner's phrase) and learning from it, I pick up nuggets of wisdom from books and pass them on to others.

Like the man with the green gravel, I skip the effort and try to pretend the results are real. And I'm even better than he is at fooling other people and myself. But unless I give up on the masquerade of growth, I'm not going to do much real growing at all. It's hard for grass to grow underneath all those rocks!

Lord, teach me to invest honest pain to achieve honest growth.

What we anticipate seldom occurs; what we least expected generally happens.
—*Benjamin Disraeli*

*M*y daughter learned in kindergarten that March 21 is the first day of spring. So she appeared in the kitchen that morning in shorts and a tank top, despite the fact that it was thirty-five degrees out and the biggest blizzard of the century had dumped eighteen inches of snow on us a week earlier. In her mind it didn't matter what the weather was like. It was *supposed* to be spring.

I do the same thing. Oh, I can usually pick out clothing that's appropriate for the weather. But I base so many of my feelings and reactions and decisions on what I think is supposed to be instead of responding to the way things really are. And too often those assumptions are as faulty as assuming a calendar day determines the weather—especially in March!

Why do I keep thinking I can really pull an "all nighter" to finish a deadline the way I did fifteen years ago? The reality is I'm older. I have more family responsibilities. I have other deadlines pending, so I can't spend all my energies on one big push.

And why do I keep picking fights with my husband because he sleeps late and I have to get up? The reality is I married a night owl who does his best work at one in the morning and whose work doesn't require him to get up early.

And why do I keep acting as if life is going to be fair, as if people are going to appreciate me the way I think they ought to, as if I will be able to tackle my problems and weaknesses without help? I know better, but somehow I keep expecting the universe to fall in line with my ideas of what ought to happen.

It's really kind of arrogant. More to the point, it's really self-destructive.

 I get a lot more done when I give up on what is supposed to be and pay more attention to what is.

I say only half-jokingly . . . that when the time comes for me to die, I will not have time to fit it into my schedule.

—Andrew Greeley

It's the flu, all right. My head feels like an oversized ball of papier-mâché. My body feels like it's just gone nine rounds with Leon Spinks *and* Rocky Balboa. I lie on the bed staring stupidly into space. Then I think I'm feeling better, so I get up and attempt to type a sentence or wash a dish. The world reels—back to bed. But inside I'm wailing, "I don't have *time* for this . . ."

I don't think anybody lives a full life anymore; everybody I know lives a *packed* life. There's no white space on the calendar. We have to schedule time for rest and play and even sex—if we don't, it doesn't happen. And something unexpected, like the flu, can bring the whole structure crashing down.

And we're not talking about frivolous activities. Most people I know have long ago pared away the nonessentials and are down to the basics: work, family, nutrition, hygiene, and an occasional sanity preserver such as a movie or a softball game.

I don't have the final answers to this ongoing dilemma, but my flu experience did give me a few insights I hope I can hang on to when the fever's gone:

- If my happiness is dependent on getting everything done, I'm going to be miserable for a good portion of my life. I've got to go elsewhere for my self-worth and for my sense of fulfillment.
- If my schedule can't survive a bout with the flu, maybe something's wrong with my schedule.
- This overload has to do with where I am in my life and with commitments that bring me joy as well as stress. There may be a time later when the nest is empty, my job has wound down, and my commitments are few. So maybe I need to thank God for my heavy schedule even as I try to find ways to adjust it.

 Dear Lord, I ask you for healing—both of my body and of my life-style. Thank you that you have blessed my life with people to love and work to do. Teach me gratitude . . . and help me find sanity.

He has made everything beautiful in its time.

—Ecclesiastes 3:11

The big oak entertainment center was my father's most ambitious project to date. A self-taught woodworker, he had put together an end table, a credenza, and other odds and ends of furniture. But this built-in cabinet, intended to house his stereo and his record collection, was much larger and more complex than any of these—and he was designing it himself.

I remember watching as that unit slowly grew to become part of our living room. First there was the clutter of rolled-up plans, then sawed boards leaning in the corner, then a long cabinet and shelves sprouting above it. For awhile, sawdust was everywhere; then the stink of varnish permeated the house. Finally the cabinet was finished, and it was magnificent—one of a kind.

What I remember most clearly, though, is that through the whole process, Dad kept messing up. He had never built a piece like that before, so mistakes were inevitable. A measurement would be off, a piece wouldn't fit, a great idea would prove impractical. And whenever that happened, Dad simply redrew his plans. He incorporated the mistake into the original design and continued building around it.

I think that's the way most of us grow. Our lives take shape bit by bit with frequent mistakes and miscalculations, often with some inconvenience and irritation for everyone involved.

The difference, of course, is that we—the works in progress—are the ones messing up. But amazingly, our Designer still knows what he's doing, even if we don't. If we let him, he can work around our mistakes and miscalculations and build them into the plan—working and reworking to shape us into something both beautiful and unique.

Lord, half the time I don't know what I'm doing with my life—even when I think I do. Thank you for being creative and persistent and loving enough to redeem my mistakes and make me beautiful.

If a thing is worth doing, it is worth doing badly.

—*G. K. Chesterton*

I was raised to appreciate fine music, but one of my favorite singers couldn't carry a tune in a bucket. He was a high-school friend, a gifted young man who excelled in art and English, earned straight *A*s, and presided over many organizations. Music was not his strong suit; he had trouble singing two consecutive notes in the same key. But he loved to sing! And I loved singing with him, because his enjoyment was so infectious. He taught me the truth of Chesterton's statement that anything worth doing is worth doing badly.

That does not mean there should be no standards or that we should do less than our best in any given area. Shoddy or lazy work is an insult to our Creator and a betrayal of the gifts he put in us. The act of doing something well can also bring great satisfaction and pleasure.

But I sometimes wonder if our contemporary emphasis on excellence is robbing us of the joy of doing things just for fun—not to mention preventing the growth that comes with trying something new. Many of us, if we aren't talented or skilled in a particular pursuit, tend to hang back from learning or even trying it.

It takes courage to do something badly and enjoy it—to dare to sing off-key, to produce clumsy paintings, or to stretch our uncoordinated muscles to play softball. But the benefits, I've discovered, are wonderful. It's hard to take myself too seriously when I know I'm not a genius—and that knowledge also makes me more tolerant of others' less-than-perfect efforts. But the chief benefit, I believe, is the built-in joy of using my eyes, using my muscles, using my voice—not because I'm good at it, but because it's worth doing!

Anything worth doing is worth doing badly—and all things are worth doing joyfully.

He will rejoice over you with gladness,
He will quiet you with His love.

—Zephaniah 3:17

When I was nine, my dad was in graduate school, and we lived in campus housing for married students. That meant concrete floors, grungy walls, wall-to-wall beds, a torn Naugahyde sofa, and no pets. But there was a big field next door where we could run and catch bugs. There was a swing set in back under a big sweet gum tree; we could swing really high and kick the sweet gum balls. And just around the corner was my forsythia playhouse.

The bush had grown large in a circular pattern spreading long, willowlike branches out from its trunk until they touched the ground a foot or so away. This created a kind of tunnel around the trunk. I could crawl in from behind and be completely out of sight behind the curtain of branches.

It was a great place to hide, to read, to play, to daydream. In winter, it was dry and crackly and protected from the wind. In summer, it was cool and green, soaked in leafy shadow. But early spring was best, when the whole bush was covered in bright yellow flowers. Even the light inside my playhouse was yellow.

It's one of my most exotic memories—spending

an afternoon in a little room made up entirely of golden blooms. Sitting there made me feel both safe and excited, free but protected—and incredibly privileged. I mean, most of my friends had more stuff than I did, but *nobody* had a playhouse made out of flowers!

Remembering that special place gives me a beautiful picture of what it means to be surrounded by God's love. I seem to spend much of my life in grungy surroundings doing what needs to be done. Whenever the grayness pulls me down, I need to stop, close my eyes and see myself as I really am— God's child, tucked safely inside his care, incredibly privileged, and utterly surrounded by beautiful, golden light.

 Dear God, thank you . . . thank you . . . thank you for loving me so much. Help me remember that, in your love, I'm still a lucky little girl.

Spring is sprung; the grass is riz—
I wonder where them flowers is?

—Old rhyme

*W*e planted beans in a little cup, watered them, and put them in a warm window to wait. Five minutes later she was leaning on the windowsill, disappointed that nothing was happening. And although I smiled at her vague concept of time, I knew how she felt.

I have spent a lot of my life in the time warp between planting and sprouting, between making my move and seeing results, between doing what I could and knowing whether I did the right thing. I apply for the job, but I won't hear yea or nay for days or even weeks. I invite a new acquaintance to lunch, not knowing whether friendship will flower. I have the biopsy, but they'll call me in a few days with the results. I work on a committee, teach a class, or pray for someone, but only time will tell whether my efforts have made a difference.

Whether it's filled with excited anticipation or fearful dread, waiting is hard. And it's especially hard when I realize that I may not see results even in my lifetime.

Something deep inside me clamors for closure. Like my three year old, I don't *want* to wait and see how the future unfolds; I want to know now! But life usually doesn't work that way. Much of the time, I'm stuck with waiting. But while I wait, maybe there are some things I need to ask myself:

- Have I really done all I can do—including pray?
- Is there something I need to learn while I'm waiting—about patience, trust, or overcontrol?
- Are there matters I need to attend to in the meantime? Is my frustration distracting me from other matters that need my attention?
- Do I need a perspective adjustment? Have I fallen into the child's trap of thinking the only reality is what happens *now?*

 Lord, Psalm 90 reminds me that "a thousand years in Your sight are like yesterday when it is past." Give me the gift of your perspective whenever I feel caught in a time warp.

Imagination [*is*] . . . *Reason in her most exalted mood.*

— *William Wordsworth*

*M*y six-year-old daughter is a spinner of tales. She loves to dream up fantasies and tell them to me. She also embellishes her factual reports. A simple report about what happened at school will gradually evolve into a delightful piece of fiction replete with unicorns.

And that poses a dilemma for me. I believe in nurturing imagination. I'm convinced we learn to solve problems in our lives by coming up with ideas that depart from what we've always done and thought. And I love my daughter's stories. Her imagination brings me delight. But I also believe in honesty, in speaking the truth to myself and others. Without honesty, our creativity is of little help in solving problems, because problems have to be faced before they can be solved.

This isn't a problem for children only. Do you ever struggle to find a balance between what is and what might be? Do you ever wonder at what point a positive attitude becomes denial or when rigorous honesty becomes hard-edged fatalism? For me, it's easy to tip the balance—to live in a dream world or to get trapped in the cynical realism of thinking things will never change.

I think the key to balance here is to realize that imagination and realism aren't the polar opposites we make them out to be. Surely honesty must recognize the power of dreams, and the best imaginative tales hold a clear mirror to truth. Imagination is best used in a way that opens up reality, not runs from it.

To help us both find that balance, my daughter and I have set up a practice of calling a "reality check" *after* the story. She's free to embellish her tales at will, but I'm also free to call for a more down-to-earth account when I need it. It's too early to know if this practice will help us keep in touch with what *is* without losing heart for what *might be*, but it shows promise.

 Dear Lord, teach me to nurture the gift of imagination without losing touch with your truth.

Coming down the hill it is delightful, cool, and pleasant. The sweet suspicion of spring strengthens, deepens, and grows more sweet every day.

—*Francis Kilvert*

It's only March, and already the magazines are pushing the panic button: swimsuit season is around the corner. Better start that diet, better get serious about your situps, better start checking out the various brands of tan-in-a-bottle.

In just a few months, they all promise, I can drop ten pounds, tone up, shape up, and find a swimsuit that will flatter my particular figure type. All I have to do is look past the chocolate cake recipes and follow their brand new, quick-shape-up plan.

But I've heard all this before, and this year I'm not buying it. Yes, I want to be trim and toned (it will take more than ten pounds). I would also like to be strong and organized and balanced. But I've grown leery of three-month solutions to lifelong challenges, and I refuse to spend my spring fixated on summer.

This has nothing to do with whether I have winter flab to lose. I do! But I am convinced that positive growth is not a once-and-for-all, get-it-done-and-get-it-over-with proposition. Growth is not a brief campaign that ends in a season of triumph. What happens *after* swimsuit season?

As I see it, growth is a daily tending in a positive direction—the kind of growth that "strengthens, deepens, and grows more sweet every day." I may need a plan to guide my decisions. And I may have—*will* have—some setbacks along the way. But I will continue making progress as I concentrate on the small, day-to-day decisions that take me in the direction I want to go. In the meantime, if I keep my attitude adjusted, I'll have the added bonus of enjoying the journey.

I'm in my life for the long haul, not for swimsuit season. I will make decisions that move me toward sweet, steady growth.

Rise up, my love, my fair one,
And come away.
For lo, the winter is past,
The rain is over and gone.
The flowers appear on the earth;
The time of singing has come.
—Song of Solomon 2:10–12

*T*t's dogwood season here in East Tennessee.

Unfortunately, it's also tax season.

Today as I drove to my accountant's office with my bulging folder of receipts, the hills beside the roadway were gorgeous. Dogwoods draped the brown and green hills with elegant drifts of white. Redbuds bloomed pink. The sun was smiling to apologize for weeks of drizzle. And I was on my way to spend another couple of hours contemplating dismal financial realities.

It seems to happen every year. I spend an entire April angry and depressed because I just don't have time for spring. I've got tax stuff to do and job stuff to do, commitments to honor and promises to keep. And this year is especially bad. Sickness and bad weather and a string of other calamities have thrown me impossibly behind.

But I hate to have spring happen without me. Neglecting to celebrate, failing to savor the beauty seems somehow shortsighted. Restricting my revelry to a passing appreciation on the way to an appointment just seems wrong.

There are long-term solutions to my April dilemma; I know that. I need to plan better, organize better, prune my commitments, limit my promises. And I really want to do better—next year. But in the meantime I've booked a cabin in a nearby national park for part of the weekend. I've marked it on my calendar—in ink. My little girl and I have serious plans to ramble in the woods.

Getting away will cost me a lot of late-night hours in weeks to come. But I'm determined not to hole up in my house, my office, or my accountant's office, and let another dogwood spring drift by me.

 Sometimes joy is a discipline and celebration is a responsibility.

When it rains it pours.

—Old saying

First it was the flu, the kind that really knocks you out. Then came the snow—eighteen inches that paralyzed this Southern town for almost a week. Then my computer blew up—not literally, but it felt that way. And I need my computer to make a living.

That was March. Next, April brought "financial disaster week." We lost the renters in the house we can't sell. The house was vandalized. A banking mistake sent checks bouncing. Then we got the verdict on our income tax. *Gulp.*

Sometimes life seems to happen like that—a raging spring flood of calamities and inconveniences. Growth takes a back seat to survival; we do what we have to do to get by. And I don't have any real wisdom to offer in this situation; I'm right in the middle of it right now. But here are the principles I'm clinging to like tree branches over white water while I wait for things to calm down. *(Help!)*

- *Lay off the blame,* of others and of myself. People are only human, and sometimes things just *happen.*
- *Don't get isolated.* Problems can build walls between people. I need to ask for help and offer it.

- *Give myself a break*. I can't expect to recover from weeks of disaster in just a few days. And all I can do is all I can do.
- *Avoid paralysis*. I can't do everything, but that doesn't mean I should do nothing. I can take steps to handle the most pressing matters.
- *Take care of myself*. Developing an ulcer or sinking into depression won't help matters, but adequate exercise, rest, and nutrition might.
- *Take joy breaks*. I need to take time to notice and celebrate the things that are going right.
- *Remember that life won't always be like this*. Please, God, say it won't!

It's a cliché, but "this too shall pass." My task is to hang on and keep growing!

If you are walking on the Decatur Road
when winter turns spring, you will
probably slip and fall and hurt yourself. It
is a mud-happy stretch at this turn, and if
you are not careful you could very well
slide all the way into Decatur.

—Joe Coomer

The old-time preachers called it *backsliding*. And that's exactly how it feels when you've made significant progress, really grown in some area, only to fall back into your old habits.

You've stuck to your eating and exercise plan, and your faithfulness has been rewarded by toned muscles and a smaller dress size. Then one day you're a slug in front of the TV, mainlining ice cream again.

You've disciplined yourself to handle each piece of paper only once, filing papers away or tossing them as they hit your desk. And you've reveled in the sense of order—until one day you put aside a paper to "think about it," and before you know it you're shuffling through a haystack of correspondence just to find an eraser.

It's an irritating and discouraging experience, but it doesn't have to send you all the way back to the mud puddle any more than a cold snap after Easter has to signal a new ice age. You always have the choice to stop your slide by reaching for help and changing your direction. And the old-time preachers had a word for that too—*repentance*.

Don't let any "holy roller" connotations get you down here. *Repent* isn't a browbeating term; it's a promise of hope. It means that with God's help, no matter how far back you've sloshed, you can climb out of the puddle and move forward again.

It's not easy. You have to face what has happened, face your own weakness, confess it to God and to others, and ask for help. It may take awhile to climb back up to where you were. But what a relief to have the chance to do it!

Lord, give me the insight to look behind the old clichés to discover truth—and hope.

So he looked, and behold, the bush was
burning with fire, but the bush was not
consumed. . . . So when the LORD saw that
he turned aside to look, God called to him
from the midst of the bush. . . .
—*Exodus 3:2, 4*

*I*t was just a little Bradford pear tree, the kind they use where I live for landscaping commercial areas. With its thin, straight trunk and its round ball of branches and leaves, it looked a lot like a tree in a child's drawing. With its three sisters, it occupied a little island in the shopping center parking lot.

My four-year-old and I were headed to the Fresh Market to grab a dose of comfort. After only six months in the city, a thousand miles away from most of my friends and family, I felt keenly the emptiness of being a stranger. I could walk all over town, and no one would recognize my face.

We got out of the car and started over to the little store whose fresh flowers, free coffee, and bakery fragrances usually made me feel welcome. And then my daughter noticed it: "Mommy, look, the tree is singing."

I stopped to look and then broke out in a smile. It was true! Evidently a flock of songbirds on their way north had decided on a layover in that parking lot. But they were all nestled deep beneath the leaves. All we saw was the pretty little tree almost quivering with their music.

It was a magical moment. The two of us stood holding hands for a long moment, listening. My daughter was entranced. And I was overcome with gratitude. For to me, the message of that tree was, "No matter where you go, you won't be a stranger to me. I'll always be here to give you even more than you thought you needed."

You see, I was looking for comfort that day. But God sent me magic!

 Lord, if you can speak through a burning bush, I guess a singing tree isn't that much of a challenge. Give me eyes to see you and ears to hear you speak.

The excessiveness of life is the best
sacrament we could ask for, a hint of how
powerful, how determined, and how
excessive You are.

—*Andrew Greeley*

*M*y part of the world is really going all out
on spring this year. Explosions of dogwoods and
redbud. Fields blanketed in wildflowers. Lawns
breaking out in an impossible, eye-popping green.
Even the bird's song is exuberant and unre-
strained—*Tweet!*

In a way, I expect spring to be energetic and
excessive. It seems normal. So if I don't take time
to listen, I might lose the message: there's nothing
inherently wrong with excess, and there's a time in
life for going all out.

I need to hear that message especially right now,
at my particular (middle-aged) time of life. Like
many people, I was an extremist when I was
young—pouring myself into my loves and my en-
thusiasms with seemingly endless energy. But as I
matured, I had to back off. I realized there are limits
to my time and my energy; I learned to assess my
resources realistically and reserve my "big guns"
for the most important battles.

The trouble is, sometimes I've gotten that message wrong. Instead of choosing my battles, I've ended up putting my guns in cold storage. At times I'm in danger of becoming too careful with myself and my energies—not reaching out, not taking risks, not investing myself fully in anything. It's easy to mistake meanness for moderation, stinginess for self-discipline, laziness for maturity, fear for wisdom.

And that's why I've got to get into my head the message of a burgeoning spring. God is a God of abundance, even a God of excess. He doesn't do things halfway. And while he wants me to grow up and learn wisdom, I don't think he means for me to back off from risk. There really are times to go all out.

God, only in your love can I learn the balance of choosing wisely but investing myself fully. Teach me the gift of excessiveness when it comes to faith, hope, love, and joy.

> *Stones and trees speak slowly and may take a week to get out a single sentence, and there are few men, unfortunately, with the patience to wait for an oak to finish a thought.*
>
> —*Garrison Keillor*

*A*cceleration seems to be the key word for this time in the late twentieth century. Everything seems to be moving faster and faster—cultural changes, unfolding events, the exchange of information, the onrush of birthdays.

To keep up, like most of my friends, I've perfected the act of doing many different things at once. I listen to tapes while I drive. I swab out the sink while I'm waiting for the water to get hot. I straighten my desk while waiting for a client to call and listen to the news while I cut up onions for dinner and talk to my daughter about school.

My days are measured, judged, by the ticking of the clock and the flap of a desk calendar. And I suspect that, most of the time, the din of passing time and the unspoken verdict of "not enough" drowns out the voice of God in my life.

It's not that God can't use the rushing events to communicate truth to me. It's just that trying to keep up with the clock and calendar does something to my hearing. I don't know if it's a secret of the universe, but so far it seems to be true in my life. If I want to remain spiritually alive, connected to the Reality that transcends time, I have to consciously slow down, jump off the time wagon. And that's not easy. I can set aside a quiet time, even make reservations for a silent weekend, and at first I'm left twitching, still ticking, unable to settle into the slow rhythm of the earth around me.

Only gradually am I learning that slowing down is not something I can "fit into" my tight schedule. That's missing the point. What I need to do is block out the hours, if necessary, and then let myself settle in, slow down, until I feel myself fitting into God's schedule. Breathe deeply. Relax with music, journaling, stretching exercises—whatever it takes. Read something that will assist the connection— meditative literature, thoughtful essays, Scripture. Or just sit and let my mind slowly settle.

And gradually the ticking and the twitching will calm down, and in the silence I may hear his voice.

 Slow time is never wasted time if I spend it listening.

Rain, rain, go away . . .

—Nursery rhyme

*I*t's one of those weeks when everybody seems depressed. Rain has been drizzling and pouring for five days straight (too many April showers). Bad news is all over the TV: a slumping economy, a virus going around, too much work for everybody. The convenience store clerk is frowning and distracted. The doctor's receptionist is irritable. My daughter is impossible. And I long to talk to someone who's openly, sincerely upbeat.

Some days it really does seem as if someone has thrown a wet blanket over the whole world. Whether it's one person's attitude or some sort of general malaise, times like that are murder to get through.

So how do we get through them? To a certain extent, of course, we need to just grit our teeth and hang on. Chances are the rain will eventually stop, people will get well, the economy will swing the other way, our hormone level will change.

But things don't always get better. Floods, depressions, wars, and epidemics really happen. Relationships sour. People turn on each other. Institutions fall apart. So I'm wary of depending too much on "the sun will come out tomorrow." Probably it will. But what if it doesn't?

I think Jesus had a much more realistic and workable approach: "In the world you *will* have tribulation," he warned, "but be of good cheer, I have overcome the world" (John 16:33). If we depend entirely on the world around us to bring us happiness and fulfillment, we'll be at the mercy of gray days and sour circumstances and the cataclysms of history. If we keep our focus on a deeper reality, we'll be able to see the rays of hope that keep shining even on the grayest days.

 God, you said there would be days like this! You also made it clear I don't have to be at their mercy. Teach me to know you, to lean on you, to focus on your light within me. (Meanwhile, if it fits your plan, how about some sunshine?)

And God said, "See I have given you . . .
everything that creeps on the earth, in
which there is life, I have given every
green herb for food." . . . Then God saw
everything that He had made, and indeed it
was very good.

—*Genesis 1:29–31*

*T*he little commuter flight took me home over a spring patchwork of blooming orchards, greening meadows, new-plowed fields—a patchwork of pink and green and brown. Delighted by its beauty, I was suddenly reminded of our wedding-ring quilt.

My husband's grandmother made it before she died—years before he and I even met. She pieced it pink and green, like the spring landscape, stitched it in patterns as elaborate and orderly as the farms and houses below me, gave it to my husband's mother with strict orders that it be given him on his wedding day.

And she left instructions, a handwritten note whose dour sternness is softened by the obvious love invested in the gift.

"This quilt is to be used as a comfort to your body," she ordered, "not to be trampled under your feet. Use it with thanks and obey God always."

I am sure she was thinking of all the lovingly stitched quilts that have ended up as moving pads, dog beds, car blankets. When I was growing up (before quilts became a valuable commodity), every family seemed to have a collection of torn old quilts that they used for a multitude of humble uses. That wasn't the fate Mama Ginny had in mind for this creation.

Now, as I see the earth-quilt spread beneath me, I muse that it was given to us with the same kind of love and the same kind of warning. The earth was given to us for our enjoyment, for our comfort, to clothe and feed us and give us joy. But implicit in the gift are the instructions that we use it and not abuse it, that we remember always the painstaking love that went into its creation, and that we always give thanks.

 Lord, you have given me this earth to walk on, but never to trample under my feet. Teach me to live on this planet with care and with gratitude.

*Seek first the kingdom . . . and all these
things shall be added to you.*

—Matthew 6:33

*T*have always been attracted by the idea of a
stripped-down life. Something in me resonates to
the idea of getting rid of the extraneous and getting
down to essentials. Part of my spirit longs for the
clear-eyed focus of the uncluttered surface, the bare
cabin, the cleared schedule, the single rose. Yet I
live among a clutter of knick-knacks, bookshelves,
paper piles, and back-to-back appointments. I
moved from a three-bedroom house to a tiny apartment and kept most of the furniture. My walls are
full. My desk is full. My life is full.

Why do I have so much trouble eliminating and
concentrating? Part of my problem involves a reluc-
tance to make hard decisions, to choose one road
and leave another behind. But I also think it comes
from the fact that the things and people and activities that junk up my life also bring me some comfort
and security. Somewhere deep is the terrified ques-
tion *If I get rid of all the clutter, will there be anything left?*

What that tells me, of course, that I'm in need
of deep-down healing—healing at the trust level.
Somehow I need to believe that simplicity doesn't
mean sterility or emptiness—that even if I'm

stripped down to my bare skin, God is still God, and God still loves me.

Maybe that's the whole point of my yearning for simplicity. It's a yearning for reassurance that there's a meaning, a relationship, a Person at the stripped-down core of my life. Once I've gotten that message, then everything else can be given to me as well.

God, you created a universe of astonishing complexity and detail. But until I trust that you are there at the core of my life, all the details will simply cause me stress. Teach me to focus on you first, then to live in simplicity, abundance, and trust.

Gold and crimson tulips, lift your bright
heads up.
Catch the shiny dewdrops in each dainty
cup.
If the birdies see you as they're passing by,
They will think the sunset dropped from
out the sky.
—Song my grandmother taught me

The snapshot is one of our family treasures. One wrinkled, ninety-two-year-old face, with a few wispy white hairs escaping from under the knitted cap. One round, rosy, two-year-old face framed in golden curls. There they are, forehead to forehead, both grinning in delight.

It had begun as a painful visit. My grandmother had been declining visibly every time I saw her. Wheelchair bound, she seemed increasingly weaker, more out of touch, sometimes lost in her own inaccessible world.

Still, we wheeled her out into the courtyard so she could enjoy the breeze. We introduced my daughter, who was curious but a little frightened by the strange, shriveled-up creature in the rolling contraption. Then we just sat and chatted while my daughter played, shyly circling closer and closer.

And then—*connection!* Light sparked in the old woman's eyes; she smiled and leaned forward. The little girl grinned and came closer. They touched foreheads and smiled at each other, friends. Dad snapped the picture.

We couldn't have engineered that moment. But it couldn't have happened if we hadn't prepared for it—if we hadn't made the effort to visit, if we hadn't bothered to bring the baby, if we hadn't brought the camera.

When I was a very young girl, that same grandmother taught me a little song about tulips who lift up their heads and catch the dew. I've taught it to my daughter. And I'm grateful that at least one time we were ready, heads up, to catch a little bit of heaven in our lives.

God, I believe you send us moments like this to help us develop a taste for your love and your wonder. Teach me to live with eyes open and head up, open to the moments of your grace.

*How can I be lonely? I'm the one in charge
of celebrations!*

—*Byrd Baylor*

It's festival time in East Tennessee (and every other place I've lived). Every little town, every ethnic group, every plant and crop seems to have its designated celebration. Through April and May, we've celebrated arts and crafts, dogwoods, azaleas, and ramps (sort of a wild onion); gardens in general and gardens in particular; Native American culture, Greek culture, English culture, Scottish culture, and Appalachian culture; two or three events of local history and three or four civil war battles; fiddle playing, gospel singing, and storytelling. If I wanted to, I could go to a party every weekend.

Part of the impetus behind the celebrations is economic. Festivals are public relations ventures, business lures, opportunities to sell to a specialized audience. And as far as I can see, they're all fundamentally alike. Every festival features food vendors, sound stages, silly contests, and souvenir tents. There are kids in strollers, Labs on leashes, young people in costumes, and racks of commemorative T-shirts.

But I'm convinced there's more going on here than fund-raising and "me-tooism." Surely these festivals began as healthy responses to a deep, God-given impulse: spring's here, the world is beautiful, we're alive—let's get together and celebrate (and eat, and dance, and wear decorated T-shirts).

Writer Charlie Shedd once quoted a psychiatrist friend as saying that one indicator of emotional health is the ability to say "Yes," "No," and "Whoopee." Well, spring weekends were tailor-made for "Whoopee." Besides, what's wrong with having a party every weekend? Maybe I'll throw one myself!

God, your love is reason enough to celebrate. Today I have you—and springtime too. What can I say but "Whoopee?"

Pray for one another, that you may be healed. The effective, fervent prayer of a righteous man avails much.

—James 5:16

*M*y husband and I don't fight often, but this one was a doozy. We didn't throw lamps and china; we didn't beat on each other or even yell—that's not our style. But we dredged up old hurts from the past. We butted our heads against deep-seated differences that we can't or won't change. We said things that were intended to hurt, and they did.

Eventually, we both calmed down, and we found some measure of reconciliation. We reaffirmed our commitment, even though we weren't wild about each other at the moment. We kissed and made up but went to sleep still troubled.

The next morning I ran into a friend. In the course of our chatting, I told her about the fight. And she said, "You know, I woke up in the middle of the night thinking about you guys, and I said a prayer for you."

That offhand comment blew me away. Suddenly I was overwhelmed with a sense of being watched over and cared for. And although that crisis is long since over—my husband and I are friends again— the memory of that prayer still warms me.

The idea of praying for people has always been a little problematic for me. I've been in religious circles where people say "I'll pray for you" in automatic response to trouble—sort of a religious version of "There, there." I may be cynical, but I don't always trust that "I'll pray for you" means anything. I don't know what your experience is; maybe "I'll pray for you" makes you even more nervous.

But I have to say that this prayer was real, and it was wonderful. To have someone think about me specifically and lovingly and offer me to God's care—what a wonderful gift! All I can say is *thank you.*

Lord, I don't always understand how prayer works, but I know you live in us as we love and care for each other. Grant me the faithfulness and sensitivity to pray for others as my friend prayed for me.

*S*he's attractive, intelligent, creative, fair-minded, kindhearted, hardworking—altogether an exemplary human being.

She's ugly, stupid, selfish, bigoted, lazy, and petty—a blot in the annals of history.

And she's me. At least, she's how I think of me.

I once read that being able to hold two diametrically opposite views at the same time is a sign of intelligence. In this case, I think it's more a case of not wanting to face the real truth about who I am.

I mean, it's appealing to think of myself as good and talented. There's a kind of romantic satisfaction in thinking of myself as irredeemably wicked—a hopeless case. But to see myself as just another flawed human being, someone who means well but cannot manage to get through life without messing up—well, that's just embarrassing.

And if I'm really honest, I have to admit that this is what the real me looks like. I am competent in some areas, gifted in a few. I care about people. I work very hard. And yet, again and again, I fail to do what I think is right. I hurt the people I care about—not necessarily out of wickedness, but out of selfishness or stubbornness or just plain carelessness.

This me is not a stellar human, not the chief of sinners, just sort of a jerk. And without some sort of outside intervention, this is the me I'm stuck with! I may be brilliant or determined or well-intentioned or all three. But I don't have what it takes, over the long haul, to escape from "jerkhood."

Thank heaven—literally—for the good news of God's amazing grace. If I let him, God has the power and the willingness to release me from both delusions of goodness and delusions of wickedness. As I depend on him, he will grow me into the specific, beloved person he created me to be—the *real* real me.

 Only by God's grace can I look at myself honestly and still live with what I see.

> *Perfect love means to love the one through whom one became unhappy.*
>
> —*Søren Kierkegaard*

They've been married forty years this spring. Overall, it's been a fruitful union—two kids, three grandkids, a sizable contingent of friends and colleagues, and a slate of satisfying accomplishments. Despite nagging worries about health and kids and retirement, they're more or less content—and proud of themselves for coming this far.

But the fight they had this week was the same fight they've had off and on since the week after their wedding.

She likes to talk.

He doesn't.

She gets her feelings hurt.

He feels pressured.

Both get irritated. Sparks fly.

Yes, they've each changed over the years. Circumstances have changed them. In some ways, they've worked at changing. Certainly they've adapted to each other and learned to work through problems. But even now there are issues they have never resolved. For the most part, they've learned to just accept—but not always.

In a sense, it's a little depressing. Surely after all

those years, they would have put those problems to bed. But in another sense, they give me hope that it's possible to persist and forgive and keep hoping even when some issues resist resolution. They remind me that it's possible to live a satisfying, full life even with unsolved problems and unresolved conflicts.

How else can we flawed human beings hope to live together?

Lord, I need both discernment and commitment for my relationships to work. Help me to know where to push for resolution and where to accept our differences.

> *Casting all your care upon Him, for He cares for you.*
>
> *—1 Peter 5:7*

*A*h-ah-ah-chooooo! For me and for many others, spring is allergy season. Drifting pollen, new-mown grass, dust-stirring spring cleaning—all have the power to reduce me to a pitiful heap of sniffling protoplasm. Years of habit cause me to explain the multitude of symptoms as "just allergies." But this is not a piddling affliction. It takes my precious time. It saps my energy. It hampers my work and my relationships.

So why do I squirm at the idea that God is deeply concerned with me and my allergies? It's hard to shake the habit of thinking that God really doesn't want to be bothered with such petty miseries. Sure, he's God of the universe, God of the major crisis. But God of my hay fever? That seems a little strange. That's like saying he's God of my constant insecurity, God of my broken ice maker . . . even God of my hangnail!

Then novelist Andrew Greeley, in his remarkable prayer journal, gently reminds me that God's love is specific and personal and passionate—big enough for a world in pain but tender enough for a stuffy nose:

While I was reading the psalm this morning—and sniffling and sneezing—I was momentarily taken by a sense of how much You love each of us. . . . You have a mother's love for the dope addict, the woman living on a machine for four years, the kid killed yesterday in a fight over a sports jacket . . . the mugger lying in wait for a victim, the overweight person hardly able to walk, the Iraqi soldier waiting in his trench. . . . You love each of us with a unique and special love. . . . You suffer when each of us suffers, an enormous amount of suffering. You are vulnerable and fragile with our vulnerability and fragility, a vast weakness. Only God could possibly stand it. . . .

I believe in that love. Either You are that way or You are not and the second option is inconceivable. Help me to understand better Your love and live in the palm of Your hand.[1]

Lord, I present my sneezing, wheezing, miserable self to you. I need you. Help me believe that you really do care.

> *The only way to get control is by giving up
> controlling. It's a paradox that's not easy
> to comprehend. But it is so.*
> —*J. Keith Miller*

*O*ut of control. Too much to do. I'm forgetting commitments, neglecting significant people and important tasks. I'm eating too much and exercising too little. That little voice inside is gasping, "Gotta get organized, gotta get in shape, gotta get moving . . ."

So naturally I take the action that is most appropriate—the one most likely to get me the results I want and need. I gripe at my husband, yell at my kid, and give unwanted advice to a friend!

Sometimes I think the most difficult task in life is learning what we can control and what we can't control—then acting appropriately. And I'm convinced that a large majority of our problems stem from getting confused about which is which.

That's true for me. When I feel unusually insecure, I end up tightening my grip on something I really can't control—like other people. I become critical, blaming, manipulative, or just extra "helpful." Then I either get slapped in the face for my efforts or I alienate the people I care about. And frustration rules because my efforts to control the uncontrollable are doomed to failure.

On the other hand, when I fail to take responsibility for what I *can* control—*my* attitude and *my* behavior and *my* spiritual commitment—life frays around the edges. Important matters slide. I let myself down, and I let others down. Self-confidence takes a nose dive.

I've been both places, overcontrolling and undercontrolling. Often I'm both places at the same time—flailing helplessly in my own bad habits while I try to eradicate someone else's, haunted by that inner refrain of "I gotta . . . I gotta." Either way, I lose out on becoming who I was meant to be.

Lord, you know what I really "gotta" do. I gotta learn to take responsibility for what's mine, not for what's none of my concern. And to do any of it, I gotta learn to lean on you.

> *April is indeed the cruelest month of the year—nature striving painfully to be reborn.*
>
> —*Andrew Greeley*

*I*t's the birth season, the season of new life. New sprouts show themselves in plowed and seeded fields. Chickies and bunnies and lambies arrive on the scene (and in the pet stores). I get visions of a Bambi spring, with birds singing and adorable little animals running to welcome each newborn addition. What a charming time for my pregnant friend to have her baby. Every little one should have an April birthday.

I'm thrilled to welcome all this burgeoning new life. But I've given birth before, and my friend's recent experience brings my own to mind. I rejoice at new birth, but I am acutely aware of how difficult and painful and messy a process it can be.

I'm not just talking about labor—although labor certainly has its moments! There's also the growing discomfort as the time approaches. (I remember a walking buddy, eight and a half months along, wishing she could just set her swollen stomach off to the side and rest for a few minutes.) There are inevitable worries and doubts that mingle with anticipation. *Will the baby be healthy? Will I be a good mother?* There's the hard work of getting everything ready, the anxiety about how you'll behave under pressure, the discomfort of recovering from this major event.

Yes, it *is* worth it, as most new mothers will tell you. But birth takes a lot out of you.

I need to remember all these difficulties whenever I'm involved in bringing new things to life. New goals, new callings, new careers are exciting, thrilling—fulfilling. But the actual process of getting them born is often painful and sometimes messy. In my experience, birthing new life calls for courage and endurance, not mushy sentiment. I will do well to remember that, as I look forward to the exciting new experiences of my life.

Lord, you went through the agony of death to give us new life, so you know just how hard bringing in the new can be. Grant us the strength we need to do our part.

Fair daffodils, we weep to see
You haste away so soon.
—*Robert Herrick*

Just a few weeks ago, the whole town seemed touched with magic. Trees bubbled with bloom. Parking lot dividers and corporate landscaping waved with tulips and irises. Vacant lots sported wildflower weeds. Even the slums were spruced up with flowers.

And now, so soon, the magic has faded. Floral confetti litters the ground around trees as branches shed their blossoms and get down to the business of being green. Parking lots are parking lots again. Vacant lots have been mowed. The slums have settled back into their everyday despair.

And it's a little sad, this fading of spring—almost like a little death in the middle of life. In such a short time the magic is set aside; life turns ordinary again.

Maybe it's an obvious metaphor, but the magic in our lives and our relationships fades too.

I remember times when romance bloomed along with the daffodils, when my newborn and I discovered together the wonder of a caterpillar and an acorn, when a new friendship unfolded in the sunshine of acceptance and shared confidence. And all that fresh loved changed, faded—either into the energetic, exhausting business of growing or the withering heat of conflict and boredom.

Some relationships shriveled. But some (thank God!) bore wonderful fruit. And that's the point, I guess.

Lord, the magic always fades. That seems to be the way you've made things. Teach me to savor the freshness of new love and new relationships but to let go of the magic with good grace and to put my energy into growing.

> *Do not lay up for yourselves treasures on earth, where moth and rust destroy and where thieves break in and steal; but lay up for yourselves treasures in heaven. . . . For where your treasure is, there your heart will be also.*
>
> —*Matthew 6:19–21*

*U*pkeep has never been my strong suit. I'm more inclined to the grand gesture, the creative sweep. I like building, organizing, whipping up from scratch, starting over. I'm less patient with tending, patching, cleaning, and putting away. My housekeeping tends to be of the "let it all pile up till it drives you crazy, then clean like mad" variety. As a worker, I tend toward the "put it off, then panic" approach.

But despite these haphazard tendencies—or perhaps because of them—I'm learning to appreciate maintenance. I'm having to face the fact that I can't always muster a successful, last-minute effort, and I don't always have time for eleventh-hour cleanups. Regular upkeep allows me to take advantage of last-minute opportunities and saves me from the humiliation of being caught in disarray. If I don't grow in the discipline of maintenance, I risk becoming tired, bitter, and defeated. In a sense, maturity demands maintenance.

But even as I work to cultivate the habits of tending, patching, cleaning, and putting away, I've got to keep perspective on *what* I'm trying to maintain. It's possible to spend all my time and my energy maintaining and defending things that I am doomed to lose anyway—things like youth and health and material possessions and even life itself. Better to concentrate my maintenance efforts on items of eternal significance—my connection with God and my relationships with other people.

 I need the disciplines of tending, patching, cleaning, and putting away. Even more, I need the disciplines of faith, hope, and love.

> *We admitted we were powerless . . . that*
> *our lives had become unmanageable.*
> —Step One of the Twelve Steps of
> *Alcoholics Anonymous*

*I*t's the one complaint guaranteed to raise my hackles: "But I can't . . ."

"I can't draw."

"I can't sing."

"I can't do math."

Whether it comes from adult or child, I bristle when I hear it. And I *hate* to have to say it! I was raised to be a "can do" kind of person. Deep down, I'm convinced I can do anything if I put my mind to it. Having to say "I can't" smells like failure to me. It feels humiliating.

And it *is* true that "I can't" easily becomes a self-fulfilling, self-limiting prophecy. (As my grandfather used to say, why would you want to prove yourself wrong?) I've seen people robbed of joy in whole categories of life because they told themselves "I can't." Sometimes "I can't" really means "I'm afraid to try," and it gets in the way of growth.

But I'm gradually learning (the hard way) that "can do" can be as damaging as "I can't." Maybe I really *can* do anything if I'm willing to make the tradeoffs. But the tradeoffs are significant, and in many cases the payoffs are just not worth it. I am a human being—subject to the limitations of talent and time and choices made. That means that in many situations, learning to say an honest "I can't" is not a form of self-sabotage but a necessary lesson in humility. If I persist in "can do" and fail to weigh the tradeoffs, I let people down, I end up feeling like a failure, and I pass up an opportunity to grow.

To rephrase the famous Serenity Prayer:

Lord, grant me the serenity to accept the things I can't . . . The courage to do the things I can . . . And the wisdom to know the difference.

*Let us eat and be merry; for this my son
was dead and is alive again; he was lost
and is found.*

—Luke 15:23-24

I don't know why I decided to look into that hole again, but I'm glad I did.

Our cat Freddie had escaped from our apartment, and three days later he was still missing. Now, this is not a tough, streetwise animal but an overweight, sheltered house cat. We couldn't imagine his fending for himself. So we worried—and searched. We called his name, put up posters, and checked at the Humane Society, Finally we gave up searching, although we still hoped he would find his own way home.

Then this morning I decided to check the little opening into the apartment-building basement one more time. And this time my call was answered with a faint meow. Within minutes I was reaching through that small opening, trying to hoist a fat (but hungry) feline four feet off the floor. Now he's sprawled as usual on the bed, all four legs in the air—and I can relax.

Okay, I know he's just a cat. But the experience of losing him and finding him helps me understand a little more personally the story that Jesus told about a father and his wayward son. The son finally slunk home after wasting his whole inheritance and ruining his life. He knew his father would disown him—but the father just wanted to celebrate!

Jesus made it pretty clear that God is like that father. We can spend our lives running from him. But when we're ready to come home, he's eager to welcome us. For the first time, in a small way, I can vouch for that. Freddie put us through a lot of worry and work, and it was pretty stupid of him to run away. But when we found him, my only response was gladness. And that makes me feel a lot better about going home myself!

 Dear Lord, you speak to me in little ways as well as large, and this week you've spoken to me through my cat. It's hard to believe you love me so much—but thank you.

God is an inveterate risk-taker.
        —*Elizabeth J. Canham*

*S*he's a sweet child, a pretty child, my daughter's best friend. And I'm a little embarrassed to admit this, but something about her gets on my nerves. It's not because she's loud or rude, but because she's so careful with herself.

When she was visiting the other day, we climbed the hill behind our apartments. I thought it would be fun to take the back way down—a little wooded path. The minute we started through the sparse underbrush, she started worrying that she would "put out an eye." Later on, we went to a playground. There, she worried about getting overheated. I have no fear of this child's being hit by a car; she won't even venture onto a parking lot. While she plays, she worries about snakes, poison ivy, and being abducted.

I have no idea why this child is so fearful. Perhaps she was sick a lot when she was younger; perhaps she has an overprotective parent. For me, however, the issue is not what her problem is but what *my* problem is. Why do I find this child so irritating? I'm afraid the answer is all too apparent: it's because she reminds me of me.

Some people are born risk takers; they love to

live on the edge. In the interest of balance—and perhaps to remain alive until their next birthday—they may need to temper their daredevil tendencies.

But people like me and my daughter's friend have a different kind of challenge. By nature, we are prone to spend a lot of energy taking care of ourselves—anticipating trouble and avoiding it, steering clear of danger, avoiding risk. In the interest of growing, we need to learn to step out, to venture forth, to take a risk when a risk is called for—trusting that God will keep us safe.

Lord, I know in my head that risking myself by depending on you is not really a gamble. Please hang in there with me while I gather up the courage to act on that knowledge.

*And lo, I am with you always, even to the
end of the age.*

—Matthew 28:20

Want to see a teacher explode?

Just try making a remark about working "only"
six hours a day—or "only" nine months a year. If
you are not injured, you'll be quickly enlightened
about what happens behind the scenes of the teach-
ing profession—curriculum development, lesson
preparation, conferences, grading, career development, and much more.

Of course, that is true of almost any pursuit; a
large portion of the work goes on behind the scenes.
Behind every corporate report lurk weeks of re-
search, writing, and emptying the coffeepot in the
middle of the night. Behind every speech hide hours
of scribbling, editing, and even declaiming before
the mirror. Behind every clean house kneels a
householder with a vacuum cleaner and a bottle of
all-purpose cleaner.

It's a mistake to assume that the only work that
counts is work that is immediately visible. But I
think I do that a lot with God. Either consciously
or unconsciously, I evaluate God's work in my life
according to whether I can see progress or feel his

presence. If I can't, I often assume he's not on the job.

But there's so much about God's work I can't see—at least not until later. What feels like intense conflict may be his preparation for a new era in my life. What feels like spiritual dryness may be his strategy for drawing me closer to him. Ordinary events may actually be a series of sacred opportunities that I'm too dull to perceive. In other words, I often can't see what God is doing in my life—but that doesn't mean nothing's happening!

And I *know* all that—so why can't I remember it?

Father, grant me the perception to see your work in my life—and the faith to assume you're working even when I can't see it.

This is the day the LORD has made;
We will rejoice and be glad in it.
                                    —*Psalm 118:24*

*S*pring's spectacular phase is over. Right now there are no cloudbursts or flash floods, no glorious, can't-stay-inside weather or breathtaking floral displays. I'm not in love—at least not at the moment. It's just an ordinary spring day—filled with ordinary activities, an ordinary husband and child, ordinary friends.

In a sense, this is the kind of day that most tries my faith, my hope, and my love. There's nothing like a good crisis to increase my energy and remind me how much I need God. There's nothing like a gorgeous day to remind me to rejoice. And there's nothing like a little romance to motivate me to be a better, more caring person. (It's even motivated me to lose weight!) But persevering through my everydays, learning to be loving and faithful and joyful day after ordinary day—now, there's a challenge!

But the Psalm tells me, "This is the day the LORD has made"—and I see no specific mention of crisis days or drop-dead-gorgeous days or days when my hormones and my heart are hopping. The Lord has made even this boring, slightly irritating day, and I am called to learn from it and to rejoice.

How? Maybe I can learn to rejoice in doing what is right even when I don't feel like it. Maybe I can learn to rejoice in subtle beauty—a sparrow's brown, mottled markings; a friend's quiet voice; the graceful pattern inside a cut onion. Maybe I can rejoice in love that takes a less gaudy form, love that shows itself as faithfulness, loyalty, and consideration. And maybe those things are more important to my growth than all the spectacular circumstances I'm motivated to rejoice about on nonordinary days.

Lord, you are God of the huge and the minuscule, the spectacular and the ordinary, the dramatic and the daily. Teach me to rejoice in every day that you have made.

> *For there is hope for a tree,*
> *If it is cut down, that it will sprout again,*
> *And that its tender shoots will not cease.*
> *—Job 14:7*

Can't be fixed: a child's face stares bleakly up at me over the plastic shards of a shattered toy.

Can't be fixed: the giant oak lies among the hurricanes debris, its roots upended helplessly.

Can't be fixed: the man and the woman stare across the distance between them, shocked into silence by brutal words finally uttered.

Some things in life can be patched up, shored up, repaired, or redone. But some wounds are too grievous, some blows too shattering, some rifts too wide to be pulled back together. Some experiences—a divorce, a betrayal, abuse, neglect—leave us permanently wounded, our psyches disfigured. We live, we go on, but we're not really *fixed*.

Yet I believe there is an alternate plan for things that can't be fixed. It won't work for shattered plastic, but this plan can make an astonishing difference in living, growing things like trees and people. I've seen it in a new shoot growing from a shattered stump, in the faces of a couple whose counseling sessions are finally showing some progress. I've seen it in people who have hit bottom and admitted their own helplessness, only to begin growing again from there.

As far as I can see, God's strategy for broken trees and limbs and lives and souls is not repair but growth, not being patched up but being granted the gift of starting over.

Can't be fixed—but can be reborn.
Can't be fixed—but can be made new.

 Lord, the older I get, the more I feel like a patched-up collection of old wounds and badly healed scars. I give you my broken pieces. And I beg you not to fix me, but to make me new again.

How lucky we are to have such a treasure of memories.

—Lady Byrd Johnson

It's not the official end of spring. Practically speaking, though, Memorial Day is the gateway to summer. School's out. Schedules change. People head for the beach and the ball field.

But many also head for the local cemetery or the Vietnam Memorial. For Memorial Day is intended to be more than the first three-day weekend of summer; it's a day for remembering. Today's paper is packed with interviews—men and women remember their wartime experiences, rejoicing in what was gained and mourning over what was lost and pondering the meaning of their experiences.

When I think of it, that's not a bad thing to do on a regular basis—to journey into memory for the purposes of understanding and instruction and perspective and gratitude.

That process has not been easy for a friend of mine who was sexually abused as a child. She has very few memories of her growing-up years. The protective mechanism that allowed her to survive also robbed her of so many important experiences. Only through extensive therapy has she been able to undertake a painstaking excavation of her memo-

179

ries—and uncovering those ugly and beautiful artifacts has helped her find peace and healing.

My dad has been writing his memoirs. Often, as he works he uncovers a forgotten bit of experience, a memory that teaches or delights him—and he is grateful to realize just how rich his life has been.

So today, I salute my own memories—happy and painful, good and bad. I celebrate past happiness for the joy it has woven into the fabric of my being. I acknowledge past pain for its lessons (some learned, some left behind) and for its gift of empathy. And I set aside this time to ask myself: Where have I been? Whom have I loved? What have I learned? What mistakes have I kept on making? Where has God's grace been working in my life?

 Lord, as I take time to remember, show me what you have to teach me from the past. Teach me to be grateful for yesterday while moving into today.

*God is great, and therefore He will be
sought; He is good, and therefore He will be
found.*

— *Anonymous*

*A*s a person who sunburns under a full moon,
I have never qualified as a sun worshiper. So now—
in this era of sunscreen—I get a certain amount of
satisfaction watching the in crowd hide from the
rays. Even now, in spring, the articles start to appear, urging us to get prepared for "sun season."

According to the article I just read, protecting
ourselves in these days of ozone depletion is a full-
time occupation. We're supposed to put on high-
octane sunscreen first thing in the morning and
replenish it during the day because it is almost impossible to hide from the sun. Ordinary T-shirts
won't keep out those UV rays. Hats and umbrellas
don't keep out reflected sun. Only a good sunscreen, applied conscientiously, offers adequate pro-
tection from wrinkles and skin cancer and "horrid"
age spots. Even with sunscreen, we're advised to
stay indoors between the hours of eleven and three.

All of this sounds a little scary—and it's a lot of
trouble. But if I turn the whole picture around a
little, I get a vivid picture of how God's love works.
We talk about seeking God, when in reality his love,

like those UV rays, is always seeking us. He is positive, powerful energy that seeks me out and helps me grow (no horrid age spots here). His love surrounds me all the time, even when I can't see it. If it can't reach me directly, it will find me another way. There's only one way I can avoid its effects—by choosing to say no to it—and even that doesn't always work.

Lord, you surround me and seek me out even when I think I'm seeking you. I want to bask in your love and mercy.

It is possible to begin again, It is hard and
we never do it perfectly, but it can be done.
—Andrew Greeley

I finally got the desk cleaned off, and I swore I would never let myself get in such a mess again. Now, as I peer through the mounds of paper, I realize I need to start all over again.

I worked hard to get in shape, and I swore I would never let myself get flabby again. Now, as I puff up the stairs, I know I need to start over with that, too.

I finally made room in my schedule for a desperately needed daily quiet time. And now, looking around with tired, panicked eyes, I realize that's gone down the tubes too. I need to start over once more.

Sometimes I get so tired of starting over. It's humiliating to face the fact that I've messed up yet another time, to go back to square one and try again. I start feeling like that old song about Michael Finnegan—where every verse ends with "begin again" and the whole song starts all over. After awhile, the repetition gets on your nerves!

But do I really think I'm going to get rid of my bad habits and self-destructive ways in one campaign, one organizational frenzy? Do I really think that one round of good intentions—or even thirty rounds of good intentions—will exempt me from making mistakes? And do I really think the only mistakes I'm allowed are the ones I've never made before?

If I understand anything at all about God, it's that his love and his grace are infinite. God is not concerned about the number of times I have to start over; God just wants me to keep growing and leaning on him. I don't have just three chances to get it right; I can begin again any number of times. Most of the time, it's my own shame and unrealistic expectations that hold me back.

For me, at least, trying again after I've failed repeatedly takes a tremendous amount of courage. It feels like a huge risk because the stakes are higher, so it requires a stronger dose of humility and grace. But maybe it can also bring me to a clearer understanding of who I am, who God is . . . and why I need God in the first place.

 Okay, God, I'm ready if you are—let's try it one more time. Remind me that I can do it only with your help. And thank you for your gift of infinite new beginnings.

NOTES

1. Andrew Greeley, *Love Affair: A Prayer Journal* (New York: Crossroad, 1992), pp. 61–62.

SUMMER

a time to enjoy

To Dad, Mom, Jer, the Avilas, and Sheahans,
for the summer stories

to Laura Frances, for seeing me through

and to Mom, for the gift of words.

Live in each season as it passes; breathe
the air, drink the drink, taste the fruit, and
resign yourself to the influences of each.
                    —Henry David Thoreau

*P*erhaps more than any other season, summer gives us the opportunity to just "be," to slow down and live, instead of merely surviving from activity to activity. For those of us with kids, summer can mean an entire three months without PTA meetings, school plays, and football practice . . . maybe even a glorious week or two when the kids are away at camp! And for those who are single and working, the longer days of summer beckon us to come home, slip into shorts and sneakers, and make the most of warm evenings spent with family or friends.

Is there a way you can resign yourself to the influences of summer? Maybe this is the time to start those tennis lessons you've been meaning to take and work up a good sweat two nights a week. Or find out if there's a drive-in theater still around and pile the family into the station wagon for a fun night out. How about inviting those new neighbors over for burgers on the patio?

Could it be that the best way to enjoy life right now is to do nothing? It's okay to do that, you know. You might even want to splurge on a new hammock, make yourself some lemonade, and spend one of these warm summer evenings suspended between two trees! Breathe the air. Drink the drink. Taste the fruit. Let go and let yourself enjoy the pleasures of the season.

Get the most out of summer.

The grass always looks greener on the other side.

Remember February? Cold, damp, dreary; bare trees and dirty snow; endless rain; cloudy days that seem to last a lifetime. You were tired of muddy boots messing up your kitchen floor, or having to wash endless loads of laundry just to keep everyone in layers of clean, warm clothes. The kids may have had fun in the snow, but you found yourself saying, "I can't wait for summer!"

Now it's summer and you're growing weary of the heat, day in and day out, with no relief in sight except for afternoon naps in the air-conditioned house. The pavement's too hot for bare feet, mosquitoes ruin the summer nights, and you actually look forward to a nice, crisp February day.

Sounds like a clear-cut case of the grass being greener on the other side! Isn't it possible just to enjoy the day that's put before us without wishing we were somewhere else?

Of course it is. But sometimes it takes a real effort to get our feelings to catch up with the truth. That's why we need to focus every day on what we've been given for this day, complete with its joys and sorrows, delights and irritations. There's a way to do that, but not without help. It's called grace, and we need it just as much when life is monotonous as when it's painful or full of pressure.

Today I will embrace what is given to me without complaining. I know that even the monotony of a long, hot summer day can remind me to take hold of the present, without wishing it away for something I think would be better.

April showers bring May flowers, but June weddings bring April showers.

It's June again, and that means weddings. Those who are in a good marriage can enjoy going to a wedding and remembering their own "happiest day." What about those who've been divorced? A wedding can serve as a painful reminder of broken vows and unfulfilled dreams.

Some may attend a wedding and feel the sharp twinge of pain from a broken engagement, a marriage that almost was. The peculiar loneliness of being single and longing for intimacy with a life partner can make it hard to rejoice in the happiness of yet another married couple.

Any of these things can make it hard to shop for a wedding gift, attend a bridal shower, or even hear the strains of Mendelssohn's *Wedding March*. Weddings are packed with emotions, whether they are pleasure, pain, or a mixture of both.

Next time you go to a wedding, focus on your emotions. Ask God to help you accept your circumstance, whatever it is.

School days, school days, dear old Golden Rule days . . .

It seems that no matter how old we get or how long it was since our last school day, June somehow brings back some of the same feelings that it used to give us, knowing that we were at the end of a long academic year. I remember those last few days of anticipation, counting the hours until we were free at last, cramming for those final exams, and looking forward to emancipation from studies. Now, as the days get warmer and the graduation greeting cards fill the store racks, I still get a sense of excitement, even though my daily work schedule doesn't change a bit.

It's no wonder that we experience a little of that considering that most of us spent twelve, sixteen, or even more of our formative years waiting for school to be out in the summer. It's a natural function of our "inner clock," and it's enhanced by the fact that we all know someone—maybe our own children—who is excited about summer vacation.

So what do we do with those feelings? Most of us experience few changes as dramatic as getting out of school, unless we're teachers or students. But can we take advantage of that "inner clock" to make some beneficial changes in our lives? How about setting out to do something different during summer vacation, like planning a weekend getaway, joining a softball team, or planting a garden? Maybe we can recapture some of that old June vitality and put it to good use.

Think about what it felt like to get out of school for summer vacation. Then write down three things you can do this summer to change your daily pattern and bring back some of that youthful exuberance. Tell somebody about it.

Let the little children come to Me, and do not forbid them; for of such is the kingdom of heaven.

—Matthew 19:14

*W*hen was the last time you took off your shoes and played in the sprinkler? Or took advantage of a summer rainshower and walked around the block, letting yourself get soaked to the skin? "I can't do that anymore; I'm a responsible adult." Yes, and you're probably missing out on the pure delight of being a kid. Watch the children next time you're in a park. Do they worry about what people will think? Of course not. That's something that we learn as we get older and gradually "put away childish things," as the apostle Paul said in the New Testament letter to the Corinthians.

Is that what Paul meant? I doubt it! Put away immaturity, maybe. Leave behind elementary ideas of faith as you grow in your journey, probably. But if Jesus Christ himself told his followers to "come unto me as little children," then there must be something to the idea of maintaining childlike wonder and spontaneity. Children respond naturally to beauty and joy, and they don't hold back when they are excited about something. They possess an inner freedom that permits them to be outwardly enthusiastic about life without fear of criticism.

Wouldn't it be great to get some of that back? What if you threw caution to the wind and took a walk in the rain, or climbed a tree for no good reason, or went to the park and hopped on a swing? Sure, you might get a strange look from somebody, but who cares? You're a grown-up, and you can do anything you want to.

Lord, help me today to see life through the eyes of a child. Instead of attempting to look perfect, help me to give myself the grace to be spontaneous and free in my enjoyment of your world.

*When a person that one loves is in the
world and alive and well . . . then to miss
them is only a new flavor, a salt sharpness
in experience.*

—*Winifred Holtby*

*F*or me, summer is a time of remembering people
I love—people who are far away because a season
of our lives is over. During June, July, and August
I can recall the in-between time at Mom and Dad's,
as a college student living in a home that was no
longer really mine, working at a summer job to
make money for next year's school expenses. Mid-
June reminds me of graduation day and saying
farewell to college friends. And the "dog days" of
late summer bring back memories of leaving friends
and family and taking a new job 2,000 miles away.

That was more than a dozen years ago, and despite the fact that I've made friends as dear as the
ones I left behind, I still miss the ones who shared
my early years. While it's true that, like the seasons,
friendships come and go, a few stay near in heart,
if not in proximity.

But it takes effort to maintain and nurture those
long-distance relationships. An occasional phone
call, a card, or a letter is like a deposit in a bank
account, an investment in caring that accrues over

time. Remembering friends in a tangible way says "you are important to me." I'm reminded of that funny little song we used to sing in Girl Scouts: "Make new friends, but keep the old, one is silver and the other's gold." Simple, maybe, but true. Friends who've known us through the seasons of our lives are worth their weight in gold, and more.

Think of one friend who is far away. Take the time today to write a little note or pick up the phone, just to let them know you miss them.

When all else fails, read the map.

One of my favorite summer activities is taking long road trips. The longer the better, and if I'm not in a hurry to reach my destination, the trip is that much more fun.

I have an old road atlas that I was given more than a dozen years ago for a cross-country trip. Sometimes, when I'm feeling restless, I'll take that atlas out and reminisce about trips I've taken and dream about trips to come. I've been doing that a lot lately! My "cabin fever" gets pretty severe during winter, and the warm days of spring and early summer start my driving foot to itching.

As I write this, I'm longing for wide open spaces and big skies, so I'm thinking about a trip to Colorado in mid-summer. How do I get there? Without looking at the map, I know I head west, but that's as far as I get. Which interstate do I take? What states will I travel through, and what cities will I visit? Are there places along the way that I'll want to see?

When I look at the map, I see that I have plenty of choices, as long as I go west. Direction is the key element in my decision making.

I suppose life is like that. In order to get where I want to go, I have to set my sights on a goal, a destination. In my case, I want to follow God's road map for my life. And that means making a lot of choices along the way. Guided by God's word, the wisdom of people I trust, and the inner workings of God's spirit, I can have confidence that I will make it to the place where I want to go.

Write down one "destination" you want to include in your spiritual journey. Share it with a friend or your spouse, and talk about how to get there.

> *At the moment, our bodies are continually responding to the messages from our minds. So what messages is your mind giving your body?*
>
> —*Margo Adair*

*Y*ikes! It's swimsuit season again. What happened? I meant to be thinner by this time! I meant to spend March, April, and May working out at the gym and eating nothing but alfalfa sprouts and raw carrots! Whoops . . . *I forgot*. I forgot that ice cream and pizza and bean burritos are not weight-reducing items. I *forgot* that sitting down all winter and spring tends to put on the pounds, and that in order to slim down, one needs to get off one's duff to see any results.

It's not that bad, really—I'm exaggerating. But the older I get, the more I realize that Sir Isaac Newton really had something with that gravity idea because gravity is taking its toll on my person.

But does it really matter? Magazines and billboards scream a not-so-subtle message that if we aren't slim and trim, we aren't desirable. If we don't have our bodies under control, our lives must be out of control. There's something wrong with us. And though this message used to be aimed at women, all you have to do is look at *GQ* or *Esquire* to know that men are under pressure to have perfect bodies, too.

It's one thing to be concerned about health, to eat things that are good for us, and to get enough exercise to keep ourselves reasonably fit. But do we have to be slaves to a cultural ideal that demands conformity? Of course not. *Just say no.*

This summer, I will try not to be overly concerned with the way I look. I will rely on God to help me withstand the pressure to be perfect.

Carpe diem—Seize the day.

$\mathcal{I}$ was captivated by those words when I first saw the film *Dead Poets Society.* If you saw it, they probably captivated you, too. Robin Williams was the boarding school English teacher, urging his students to look into the faces in the faded photographs, the ones who had gone before them many years ago. *"Carpe diem,"* they are saying—"Seize the day."

I remember a summer day just a few years ago. I was sitting at the top of the stairs in the Kansas farmhouse where my father, his father, and his father's father all lived. Now a fourth generation is growing up in that house, and my little cousin Angela is one of those lucky ones who treads the same oak stairs our ancestors trod.

Angela may be young, but I think she understands what *carpe diem* means. At the top of those stairs, we sat together as she showed me a framed sepia-toned photograph of our great-grandmother and her family. "Her name was Sarah Scott," Angela reminded me, pointing out a young woman wearing a stiff Victorian collar and high-button shoes. "My sister is named after her."

Does Angela hear the voices, through the generations, over the years? She might not be able to articulate it that way, but I think she does. Can you "hear the voices" of your ancestors? Can you look into their ancient eyes and see the dreams they had for you?

Find a picture of one of your forebears, someone you never knew. Look at the face and imagine what his or her life was like. Then write a note to a future descendant of yours, telling him or her something about you.

*Perseverance. Your own built-in
taskmaster. The thing that makes you
stick with a job until it's done.*

Summer, I believe, is the worst season of the
year for timely completion of tasks. Summer is
the time when you take your shoes off as often as
possible, leave work as early as possible, and head
for the lake or beach as soon as possible.

What seems less than possible, at least for me, is
getting things done. I'd much rather swim, play
softball, sit on the porch, hike up a mountain, mow
the yard—anything but sit at a computer screen.
So what do I do in this laziest of seasons when a
project glares at me from across the desk? I usually
succumb to temptation, especially if it involves ice
cream.

But there is this thing called perseverance. It's a
quality I've been short on most of my life, which is
why summer school was never a good idea for me.
Part of not persevering is the fear of the task, which
for buttoned-down, straight-line, Type A people is
usually not the issue. For those of us a little to the
right brain of Type A, fear of the task can grow
until the task itself takes on gargantuan proportions.

Perseverance doesn't listen when the task is

growling—it just keeps on doing what needs to be done.

The quote at the top of the opposite page was clipped out of a magazine and given to me by my seventh-grade English teacher, Mrs. Dummler. She found that and thought of me. I guess I must not have been finishing my tasks very well. I don't have the clipping anymore, but I've never forgotten what it said and what its existence said about Mrs. Dummler as a caring teacher.

Guess what, Mrs. Dummler? I finally wrote a book.

I will stick to my important tasks today and get them done. Then I'll give myself a pat on the back.

Hold a true friend with both hands.
—Nigerian proverb

*C*an you remember your first friend? Mine was a little dark-haired girl named LeeAnn, whose parents owned the beach cottage next-door to ours. I spent my earliest summers in that beach house in New Hampshire, and having LeeAnn as a playmate made those summer days just that much more fun. I've seen a picture of the two of us, tanned from long afternoons in the sun, bundled in sweaters to protect us from the evening chill as we played on the seesaw down by the water.

But even though LeeAnn and I were buddies, we couldn't possibly know what it meant to be a real friend. Life wasn't complicated enough to require that kind of relationship yet. Even so, I learned what real friendship was all about from my mom and her friend, Hilda, one warm night there at Hampton Beach. Friends since high school days, these two women strolled along the beach with their children in tow and talked for what seemed like hours. After a long day at the beach and an extra long walk down the boardwalk, I was pooped. Wasn't Mommy tired?

Not tired enough to miss out on some special time with her friend. So us kids got put to bed and left with Grandma while Mommy and Hilda went for yet another walk. I didn't understand it then, but it left its mark on me. These days, Mom and Hilda have to make do with letters because years go by in between walks on the beach.

As for me, I've taken a lot of long walks on the beach with special people in my life. Now I stay up late and talk with dear friends whenever possible. I guess I have Mom and Hilda to thank for that.

Do you have a friend you'd like to stay up late with and talk to? Do it, if you can. Or call that friend and let her or him know you wish you could.

> *Today a new sun rises for me; everything lives, everything is animated, everything seems to speak to me of my passion, everything invites me to cherish it.*
> —*Anne De Lenclos*

I am drawn to people who have a real passion for life, a zest for adventure, and a flair for spontaneity. I like to live life on the edge, dance in the street if I hear a brass band, let the ice cream drip on my chin, eat watermelon with my hands and spit the seeds out afterward.

I like to have fun and to find it in the moment instead of looking for it elsewhere. I love to drink deep of earth's pleasures, talk about the meaning of life over a cup of tea or strong coffee, and pray and laugh with equal abandon. I want to be moved to tears by the rhythm of well-written words, to laughter by the timing of well-delivered comedy, and to action by the fervor of a well-preached sermon. I love the feel of the wheel, the hum of the engine, and the view from the open window. I brake for historical markers, old barns, and bunny rabbits with white cotton tails. I sing of mountains, oceans, and tender hearts. And when I go to the beach, I couldn't care less if it's raining—I will run and dive headlong into the waves, laughing all the way.

Come, play with me, and you are a kindred spirit and friend for life.

Do you know what you love? Have you ever written it down? Take the time to do it—find out what a delightful person you are.

I am a terrific person to know! Before today is through, I will take some time to write down the things that make me unique.

Laissez bon temps roulee—Let the good
times roll!

One of my favorite summer events is something called the Golden Scoop. As you can imagine, this is an event that has something to do with that most sublime pleasure of summer: ice cream. My friend Billy, a certifiable ice cream addict (and a man after my own heart), offers his home, his boat-shaped wooden deck, and his collection of antique ice cream scoops to a circle of his closest friends. It happens every year in June, and though I am sworn to secrecy on the details of the Golden Scoop ceremony, I can tell you that it is a celebration that the F.O.B. (Friends of Billy) look forward to with great anticipation and delight.

Oh, there are grilled hamburgers, of course, and baked beans and potato salad. This is an official summer event, you know. But the high point of the evening is the ceremony, which is carried out with much pomp and silliness and serves to officially usher in the beginning of the ice cream season. Mind you, it would be great to have homemade ice cream, even without the party and the hilarity of the sacred ceremony. But it wouldn't be a celebration, and that's what makes it so special. I am glad to have friends who consider celebration to be such an important part of life. Whether the event honors a significant milestone, like a job promotion or a wedding engagement, or just commemorates the beginning of ice cream season, it's always accompanied by exuberant toasts, blessings, and sometimes a song or two. It's terrific!

Do you "celebrate the moments of your life?" Next time you've got something to celebrate, have a party.

Celebrations bring joy to life. I will take the time to celebrate even the small things this summer.

Living things need room to grow.

Having come from a long line of farmers, I have a built-in affinity for growing things. I'm not much of a gardener, mind you, but my little suburban vegetable patch can still teach me a lot about life from a farmer's perspective. There are parables to learn from every trip out to the patch . . . every time I plant, water, yank weeds, or pull new vegetables from the ground.

One such parable I learned from Bell peppers—really! The instructions on the little white stake tell you exactly how far apart to plant the peppers for maximum growth. Put them too close, and they choke each other, with roots tangled and leaves fighting for space to grow. Plant them too far apart and you've wasted a lot of space, so you won't enjoy as many peppers. But plant them just right and they'll have enough room to spread their little stalks to the sun, enough area to absorb the rain, and a healthy share of the soil's nutrients below the surface.

Like the peppers, relationships need space to grow. Do you feel choked because someone wants to be too close? Maybe you're the one doing the choking. It may be a romantic relationship, a friendship, or a family relationship. For whatever reason—poor self-esteem, a desire for control, or unsatisfied emotional needs—relationships may get entangled to a point where those involved are dying instead of growing. And the disentangling process can be very painful, sometimes to the point of having to reach down and tear out roots in order to replant. How much better it would be to be planted together with enough room to grow in the first place!

I will give thought to my closest relationships. Do I have plenty of growing room? If not, I will think about ways to create healthy space.

Earth's crammed with heaven
And every common bush afire with God;
But only he who sees takes off his shoes,
The rest sit round it and pluck
blackberries.

—Elizabeth Barrett Browning

*I*f you've never read the book, then maybe you've seen Cecil B. DeMille's epic movie *The Ten Commandments.* Do you remember the scene when Moses went to the top of the mountain to meet with God? Moses met the Almighty in the form of a burning bush, and he was informed by the voice of God that where he was standing was holy ground. His response was that of reverence, awe, and holy fear; he took off his shoes.

The Japanese know about reverence and respect; they take off their shoes when they enter a house. It's not something we Americans do out of any particular courtesy. if we do it at all, it's to be comfortable or because our feet hurt. I love what Browning says in her poem. All around us is God's creation, earth crammed with heaven. Do we really respect it, revere it, and hold it in awe? Or do we simply take it for granted?

We live in a time of great awareness of Earth's frailty. Some say that if we don't do something radical, we won't be able to pass on all its beauty to our descendants. Most of us do more than ever to make adjustments to help the earth—recycling, buying eco-friendly products, and generally "thinking green."

Some take concern for the environment to the extreme by worshiping nature. As a Christian, I can't buy that. But to revere the earth and its beauty as the wondrous work of God, to honor its loveliness with awe—that's something I can take my shoes off for.

 O Lord, I will respect the earth out of gratitude for its beauty and wonder.

The mere sense of living is joy enough.
—Emily Dickinson

*T*am fortunate to have a veranda where I live. It's an upstairs porch really, but "veranda" makes me sound like Scarlett O'Hara, doesn't it? I live on a quiet little street where most of the houses were built in the 1930s. Back then, they didn't have air conditioning, which is why houses had porches. Families could sit outside on summer nights when it was too hot to be indoors. That made for much conversation and the telling of stories because there's not much else to do when you're sitting on a porch. Rocking chairs and porch swings were places to "sit a spell" and visit.

Being out on the front porch gave you a connection to your neighbors—after all, they stepped off their porch, down their front walk, up the sidewalk, and to your house. Walking down the street in the evening, you could greet neighbors sitting on their porches, and maybe stop to have an iced tea and catch up on the latest news.

It's still that way in my neighborhood. I suspect that people who choose to live in old houses with front porches do so because they like to sit on them in the summer and talk to the neighbors.

I imagine that all of us, whether we have one on

our house or not, know the pleasure of porch-sitting. Maybe it was Grandma's house, or that big lodge up in the mountains, or that old place by the lake. It's hard to beat the feeling of just sitting and rocking and letting the world go by at a slow pace. You don't have a porch? What a shame! Get yourself a couple of rocking chairs and pretend.

I'm going to find a porch somewhere and sit this weekend with a friend or a neighbor.

*Red and yellow, black and white, they are
precious in his sight. Jesus loves the little
children of the world.*

—Children's Song

Growing up in the 1960s, I was very aware of
the fact that our country was undergoing a great
change. I saw the coverage of the Watts Riots on
TV during the long, hot summer of 1965. Images
of the civil rights marches in Birmingham and
Montgomery and the unforgettable "I Have a
Dream" speech by Martin Luther King, Jr. gave
my young mind the sense that I was experiencing
history in the making.

What did it mean to me in my daily life? I was
a white child in a white middle-class neighborhood
with virtually no contact with people who weren't
like me. Mom and Dad taught me that I was no
better than anyone else and that God loved us all
the same, no matter what color our skin was. Still,
I'll never forget one summer afternoon at the community pool. It was one of those scorching days
when it seemed as if every mother within ten miles
brought her kids to swim, so the pool was crowded
and noisy. That is, until the "Negroes" showed
up—a young mother and two boys about my own
age. I watched from the side of the pool as the boys
slipped out of their T-shirts and into the water.

I shiver when I recall what happened then. Parents motioned to their children to get out of the water, and older kids moved away from the two black boys, leaving them to splash in the water alone. And I recall having this thought: *Will that color come off in the water? I don't want to get any on me.* I'm horrified now to think about it. But I was just a child, and the idea of black skin was strange to me. Three decades later, it makes me wonder, *Do I still harbor any hidden fears and prejudices?* I'm afraid so. Maybe it won't be that way for my kids. At least I hope so.

As I go through my day, I will take notice of my unspoken thoughts and attitude toward those who are different from me, and I will purpose to change the things that are unjust.

Then God saw everything that He had
made, and indeed it was very good.
—Genesis 1:31

I've never really thought about what season it was when creation happened. Did the universe begin during the winter, spring, summer, or fall? Or did all the season stuff happen later? Regardless of how you explain the origins of the world, it's kind of fun to hypothesize about what season it was when Adam and Eve were hanging out in the Garden of Eden. I think I can make a pretty good argument for summer, actually. Think about it! It couldn't have been winter because Adam wouldn't have been able to name all the animals. The bears would have been hibernating. And fish are mentioned rather frequently in the story . . . well, you remember that old song, "Summertime, and the livin' is easy, fish are jumpin' and the cotton is high." I rest my case. Not to mention the fact that the first couple were running around buck naked. When is it warm enough to do that, besides summer?

Have I made my point? I realize that there is no mention of watermelon being the forbidden fruit (I don't think God would do that!), and there weren't enough humans around yet to get up a baseball team, but I think Eden sounds like a summer place.

If you're like me, there are probably times during summer when you think you are in paradise, like when the cool breeze comes across the ocean or when the scent of honeysuckle wafts its way onto the front porch on a warm July night.

Ah, creation. Summer showcases it well. And even we can see that it is good.

 I will take notice of creation today, and find reasons to agree with God about its goodness.

Familiarity breeds contempt.

Where I grew up, summer meant zucchini. That innocuous little dark-green squash, full of vitamins and minerals, high in fiber, low in fat. Good flavor and good for you. Look for it in the store in January, and you'll pay dearly for all that nutritional value. But come July, if you live in a zucchini-producing area and your neighbors have more than a two-foot square patch of garden, they'll be paying you to take it off their hands.

Forget the fertilizer. Zucchini sprouts forth in great abundance with no help at all. I'm not sure you even have to water it. If you aren't careful, you can grow one as big as a tuba. "Hi, neighbor! How about some fresh zucchini? Just picked it!" Gee, thanks. Mom knew how to cook it, fortunately. Fried zukes, steamed zukes, zucchini bread, zucchini milkshakes . . . you get the picture. By August, if you saw the neighbor coming up the walk with a bulging paper sack, you locked the door and pretended not to be home.

Isn't it funny? In January, we craved fresh zucchini and complained about how expensive it was in the off-season. By the end of the summer, we didn't want to see another green squash as long as we lived.

That's how it is with everything. If we don't have something, we want it. We crave it. Then, when we get it, we lose our desire for it. And if we get too much of it, we soon tire of it and begin to despise it. We've done that with things like a job promotion, recognition, or a relationship. Seems that the rarer something is, the more we value it.

How about some zucchini?

Lord, I will be satisfied with what I have, when I have it.

Sometimes the hardest work to accomplish on a summer's day is the mere act of staying at the task at all, when everything in nature beckons you to come outside and play.

*I*f it weren't for summer rain, I might starve to death. Being self-employed, I'm my own boss, which means that I tend to give myself time off when I need it . . . and sometimes when I don't. When it's clear and warm outside, sometimes it's all I can do to sit down and make myself work. I'd much rather look at the sky and the trees than stare at a computer screen, trying to come up with words. I'd trade my desk for a bike in a heartbeat.

I don't feel that way about winter, unless there's snow falling, in which case I will drop whatever I'm doing. To heck with deadlines! There are snowballs to be thrown! But those days, fortunately for my livelihood, are few. Summer, though, is a different story. I find myself hoping for terrible heat and humidity, so that I won't be tempted to abandon the day's project and head for the park, the pool, or the porch. On fine summer days, when the sky is cobalt blue and there are just a few puffy clouds, every fun thing I've ever done during the months of June, July, and August crowds my mind and screams to be repeated. Let's go to the lake and ski! Get in the car and drive to the beach! Ride bikes in the country! Hike a mountain! Wash the car!

Wash the car? Hey, I'd rather do that than stay inside and work. Wouldn't you?

 Can you play hooky from your tasks today, even if for just a few minutes? If not, take five minutes and daydream about something fun you could do if you were outside.

Everybody needs his memories, they keep
the wolf of insignificance from the door.
— Saul Bellow

Memories are crucial to our existence. Without them, we wouldn't know who we are. Memories give us our own personal history, a history that defines us and gives substance to our being.

But not all memories are good ones. Most of the pain we carry in our daily lives has its roots in memory. For one, it is the memory of sexual abuse by a family member. For another, the memory of a parent who drank too much or was unpredictable in behavior. And for some, the absence of memory is just as significant—the lack of positive interaction with an absent father, perhaps.

Some of us live with the regret of youthful mistakes—having sexual experiences before we were ready, mistreating our bodies with drugs or alcohol, or just wasting time. Even yesterday's mistake is now a memory and part of our history.

As painful as memories can be, they can also be the stepping stones for personal growth. Talking about them with a friend or counselor can help release the grip bad memories often have on our lives. Many times we're not even aware of the hold our memories have on us.

Do unpleasant memories haunt you? Do you find yourself stuffing painful thoughts away that you'd rather not remember? Do yourself a favor and begin to explore that part of your life. It's not easy, but it's worth it in the long run.

Although it is difficult, I will begin the process of opening up with someone about my painful memories.

> *As Lightning to the Children eased*
> *With explanation kind*
> *The Truth must dazzle gradually or every*
> *man be blind.*
>
> —*Emily Dickinson*

I never really appreciated lightning until I moved to the South. For one thing, it was a rare occurrence in California where I grew up. Once in a while, on a visit to the Midwest, I saw the plains light up with summer storms. And I recall that it was scary, especially because it was always accompanied by loud crashes of thunder. It was the kind of thing that sent kids scurrying for Mom and Dad, usually in tears.

I suppose it helped, hearing that it was "only thunder" or "only lightning" and that it wasn't going to get me. The older I got, I was better able to understand the scientific explanation that lightning had something to do with electricity. There was usually a history lesson with the explanation, something about Benjamin Franklin and a kite with a key attached to the string. You remember that, don't you?

But do you understand it? I don't. Oh sure, I can find out all about the electrical fields and climactic conditions and all that stuff. But there's so much mystery to it. I like the Bible's explanation better—about thunder being the voice of God. I don't doubt that for a minute!

What is the truth about lightning and thunder? And how is it that it can be so beautiful, awe-inspiring, and dangerous all at the same time?

Why is there lightning? Why is there love? And pain? I suppose that we won't know the answers to the big questions of life. And that's fine with me.

I can be satisfied with the wonder and mysteries of life, without knowing the answers to all its questions.

> *Do not withhold good from those to whom*
>   *it is due,*
> *When it is in the power of your hand*
>   *to do so.*
>
> *—Proverbs 3:27*

I just want you to know that your child was delightful in the nursery this morning." "You have a wonderful way with people, and I admire that." "Your house is so warm and welcoming." "You told that guy the truth on that deal, and I respect you for it."

Wouldn't it be great to hear things like that all the time? How many times do you think about saying something encouraging or uplifting to someone else, but you just don't feel comfortable? It's a risk; what if they think you're just trying to butter them up? You could come off sounding insincere. So you keep it to yourself, instead, and the encouraging word never gets said. Oh, maybe you think about it later and have every good intention of writing a note, but you never get it written. Time goes by and you've lost that moment forever.

It's not just words, of course. There are times when you might see a situation that could use something—time, money, skills—that you possess and could share. It might be as simple as offering to drive an elderly neighbor to the store or washing a friend's car when they're too busy to take care of it. Or it might be a case where you have extra money and know of someone who's struggling financially. What a joy to send an anonymous gift!

Think of the times that someone has given you something right when you needed it—an encouraging note or phone call, a helping hand with a project, or a few bucks when you were strapped for cash. It meant a lot to you, didn't it? Don't miss the opportunity to give to someone else.

Show me, Lord, how I can give of myself to someone else today.

Listen to this, O Job;
Stand still and consider the wondrous
works of God.

—Job 37:14

I'll tell you where I'd like to be right now . . . either standing on a peak in the Rocky Mountains or at the shoreline of the Pacific Ocean. Doesn't that sound wonderful? Getting away to a place where nature is right out in front of us can really help to clear our minds of all the stuff that clutters and keeps us from being focused. And it seems to be so much easier to focus on God when we are someplace like the mountains or the beach. The Rockies and the Pacific Ocean would sure qualify as "wondrous works of God," don't you think?

No matter what our religious background, built into each of us is an inward sense that there is Something or Someone bigger than us. In Twelve Step groups, members call on their Higher Power. In the book of Job, God's characteristics are renumerated as Job's friends attempt to counsel him through his trials. Notice that the friend in the story tells Job to "stand still and consider the wondrous works of God."

It's easy to stand still when you're gazing at the Pacific Ocean or breathing mountain air. It's tough to do it when you're in the middle of a crazy work day or surrounded by the demands of a family. But aren't those things also the wondrous works of God? The innocent face of a child, the familiar voice of a spouse, the steadiness and reliability of a co-worker—all these things remind us that we are not alone, that Someone greater is at work in the midst of us. That's a good thing to hold on to when the going gets rough.

 Today I will "stand still," if only in my mind, to consider the wondrous things around me.

When life gives you rain, make doughnuts.

know, it's kind of a goofy twist on "When life gives you lemons, make lemonade," but I like this one better. That's because it really happened, more than once, and it taught me a lesson about adjusting to adverse circumstances. When I was little, we spent quite a few summers at a delightfully ramshackle beach cottage, delightful especially because it was named after me! Our time in that cottage was limited, mostly because my brother and I would get very antsy if we weren't taken down to the water every day. So from morning until sundown, with maybe a break for lunch, those summer days were spent playing in the waves, collecting shells, and building sand castles.

Unless, of course, it rained. Then what? We didn't have a television (for which I am now thankful). I have a hunch Grandma prayed that it would rain so we would stay indoors. "Kids, would you like Grandma to make some doughnuts?" Would we! She'd let us help roll out the dough with her big, wooden rolling pin, and then we'd cut the doughnuts out with the tin mold and drop them carefully into the hot oil. When they cooled, Grandma put them into a paper bag with some sugar and we would shake them until they were covered. Funny how eating a half dozen of Grandma's doughnuts could make an eight-year-old forget about the beach.

Grandma's been gone for years now, but I'll never forget how she could transform a rainy day into something wonderful. And I think I need to get that recipe from Mom.

If I am caught in unpleasant circumstances, I can come up with creative ways to turn them around.

> It hain't no use to grumble and complain,
> It's jest as easy to rejoice;
> When God sorts out the weather and sends
>   rain.
> Why rain's my choice.
>
> —*J. W. Riley*

The morning is rainy where I live, and though I prefer sunshine to rain most days, I'm aware of rain's purpose in creation. Where I live, spring and summer rains are frequent, and the landscape shows its lovely greening effects in the light hues of spring to the darker shades of August. Trees are leafy, good for providing shade on a hot, bright day. If you've seen pictures of Ireland, you know how green it is over there. I found out why when I visited a few years back. It rains almost every day, even in the summer. But it's rarely torrential or violent. Often the rain comes down in gentle showers or mist, what the Irish call "soft" days.

Rain does soften the day and quiet the world. Sun is loud—it just calls for shouting. Notice the birds; even they are quiet when the rain falls.

Now, I'm one who enjoys a boisterous summer day, with children laughing and birds chirping and even cars honking. But it's nice to have a rainy day every once in a while. It's a good time to get quiet, to be reflective, and to slow down just a bit.

What happens to you on a rainy day? Do you see it as an intrusion, as a foiler of plans or an inconvenience? Or do you accept a rainy day as God's way of getting you to slow down? Rain waters the grass and makes the flowers grow. Can it give some refreshment to your spirit?

 Instead of complaining about the rain, I will be thankful and appreciate the way it quiets my world.

Begin to weave, and God will give you the thread.

—German proverb

Some people take great joy in beginning a project. They lay out their tools, line them up neatly, outline the tasks, and set a precise schedule for the work to be done. Then they begin and methodically work through each stage until they finish.

Maybe you're like that, but I'm not. Beginning anything is the worst part because when it comes right down to it, the hardest thing for me is to jump in there and do the first thing on the list.

It just looks so big! And that's any project, whether it's an article to write, a kitchen to clean, or a list of people to call. The task looks enormous, and it threatens to overwhelm me. I'll never get the whole thing done, will I? I'm so thankful that I came upon this little saying: "How do you eat an elephant? One bite at a time." And why? Because there have been too many times in my life when the elephant has eaten *me*. When a task or project is too daunting, I can easily curl up in a little peanut shape and be chomped under the tusks, if you get the picture.

What about you? Is the elephant eating you or are you eating the elephant? It doesn't take much to become a meal for a mammoth. Fear and anxiety rob you of the strength you need to get under way with any task. Mind you, I don't have a handle on it yet, but it's getting better as long as I remember to take it one bite at a time. Besides, trying to eat an elephant at one sitting can make you really sick.

When faced with a project that is overwhelming, I will not be defeated. Instead, I will find satisfaction in completing each small step, until the job is done.

*Don't worry about what you missed. You
can go back and get it next time around.*
—*Charles Wells*

Have you ever seen a combine? It's a piece of
farm equipment that combines several functions
necessary to the harvesting of grain—reaping,
threshing, and winnowing. As the machine drives
over an area of wheat, for example, sharp blades
cut the heads off the stalks, and the heads are transported to the rear of the machine, where the chaff
is winnowed away and the remaining kernels of
wheat are conveyed into a holding bin in back.

I sound like a farm girl, don't I? I'm not, but my
dad was raised on a farm, as was his dad before
him, and on and on back through the generations
on that side of my family. So I guess you could say
farming is in my blood, which is why I wanted to
learn to drive a combine. Fortunately, my farmer
uncles were kind enough to oblige me.

It's not easy; a combine doesn't exactly steer like
a car, and it's about five times as bulky. And what
looks like a flat wheat field often has little bumps
and rises in it, which makes the combine weave and
shake. Trying to catch all the wheat while cornering
is tough for a rookie farmer like me, which meant

leaving wide swaths uncut—not a good thing when every kernel means cash.

But my uncles didn't worry about my crooked paths and the precious wheat I left behind. "You'll get it next time," they said. "Just adjust your steering and you'll pick it up."

Sounds like a healthy way to look at life. We can be pretty hard on ourselves if we make a mistake. Wouldn't it be great if we could encourage ourselves and each other that way?

 Today, I'll give myself the freedom to make mistakes, knowing that I can go back and do it right the next time around.

He deserves paradise who makes his companions laugh.

There's nothing better than a good laugh. Don't you love being around people who see humor in everyday life? We need to laugh. Even medical science tells us now that laughing is good for us; it releases endorphines, chemicals that get the blood flowing and increase our general sense of well-being. In totally unscientific terms, it feels darn good! Author Norman Cousins wrote about the healing power of laughter in his book *Anatomy of an Illness,* in which he related his battle with disease and his self-administered treatments of Marx Brothers movies and "I Love Lucy" reruns.

You and I may not need a cure for a physical illness, but what about a cure for the summer blahs? Stuck in an office or at home with the kids, sometimes it's hard to see the humor in daily life. Children, of course, can be a great source of laughter. When your kids say something funny, do you let go with a belly laugh or do you hold back? In your work, are you around people who automatically see the funny side of a situation? What about you? Would you be described as someone who has a good sense of humor?

I love what Reinhold Niehbuhr said about laughter. He was an acclaimed theologian, one of the twentieth century's greatest thinkers and the originator of what has become known as the "Serenity Prayer." His advice to those who sat under him? "All you earnest young men out to save the world . . . please, have a laugh."

Isn't that great? We can get so serious about life sometimes that we can wear ourselves—and each other—out. What's your H.Q. (Humor Quotient)? If you're reading this, chances are you're taking a serious look at your own life. That's great. Just let yourself laugh your head off from time to time. Nobody has ever died from an endorphin overdose.

 Today, I'll laugh if I feel like it and I won't hold back. I will look for and appreciate the people who make me laugh.

*"On with the dance, let joy be unconfined"
is my motto, whether there's any dance to
dance or any joy to unconfine.*

—*Mark Twain*

I go absolutely nuts when I feel summer coming on. I can't wait until it gets warm enough to wear shorts, and the ice has barely melted off the driveway before I kick off my shoes and go barefoot. I play my stereo several decibels louder between May and October. I drive with the windows down (even if I have to turn the heater on at night) and sing at the top of my lungs. I'm inclined to go a few miles out of my way to "be in the neighborhood" of the local Dairy Dip, just to get a chocolate cone.

What is it about summer? Is it just the weather? That's a lot of it for me. I struggle through the bone-chilling grayness of our long winters. But there's a freedom about summer that just doesn't exist at other times of the year, even during the soft, cheerful spring or the clear crispness of autumn.

Could it be that we can interact with nature in ways that weather prohibits (or at least discourages) at other times? We can run headlong for the surf and dive through a wave, and the cool that greets us is refreshing to body and soul. Flopping down on the sand after a good swim, we feel the tingle of the warm sun against chill-bumped wet skin. Hiking a mountain trail in summer, we work up a healthy sweat and splash ice-cold water on our faces.

Is this making you want to jump up and do something fun? I hope so! There's a lot of joy to be found in summer's pleasures. Let it be unconfined!

Finding joy in small things is a happy, healthy way to live. I'll try it today.

I grow old . . . I grow old . . .
I shall wear the bottoms of my trousers
   rolled.
Shall I part my hair behind? Do I dare to
   eat a peach?
I shall wear white flannel trousers, and
   walk upon the beach.
I have heard the mermaids singing, each to
   each.

— *T. S. Eliot*, "The Love Song
   of J. Alfred Prufrock"

*G*rowing old is something we all think about. For some of us, those thoughts come more frequently. It's easy to think you're eternally young if you're slim and trim, with a head full of hair. But when those laugh lines around your eyes turn into crevasses and the hair on your head turns silver (some of us wish we had hair at all!), then we're forced to face the reality that we're not teenagers anymore.

Maybe we're seeing the aging process take its toll on our own parents. In our minds, Mom and Dad might be thirty-five, but when we see them now we recognize our grandparents in their maturing faces. Acknowledging that makes us mindful of the fact that we, too, will one day be eligible for senior citizen discounts.

Think about the kind of person you'd like to be

twenty, thirty, or forty years from now. Cultivate those life habits and character qualities now. As for me, I hope I'm like J. Alfred Prufrock, walking down the beach wearing rolled-up trousers. I'll dare to eat a peach, and I hope I can hear the mermaids singing, each to each.

Life is a great adventure, from first to last. Help me now, Lord, to become who I'd like to be when I am old.

> *Think enthusiastically about everything,*
> *but especially about your job. If you do,*
> *you'll put a touch of glory in your life. If*
> *you love your job with enthusiasm, you'll*
> *shake it to pieces. You'll love it into*
> *greatness, you'll upgrade it, you'll fill it*
> *with prestige and power.*
> —Norman Vincent Peale

*D*o you remember your first job? It was your first taste of real responsibility, of having to be at a certain place at a certain time, of working hard to please a boss who wasn't a parent or teacher. And at the end of the week, there was a real reward—a paycheck with your name on it!

My introduction to the working world was a summer job. It was 1973, and the minimum wage was $1.35 an hour. For that princely sum, I stood behind the counter of Mike's Hero Sandwiches and churned out salami masterpieces all summer, wearing a red, white, and blue outfit to boot. And I learned things that have served me well over the years, things like pride in workmanship (I made the *best* salami sandwiches in town), getting along with co-workers, making the customer happy, and putting a little extra effort into each task—even the boring ones.

Got the summer sluggishness at work? Maybe

it's time to remember what that first summer job was like. No doubt you've changed professions since then, but aren't you still the same person, eager to please and anxious to do well? Remember that whatever you do, no one can do it with your unique style and panache. I'll try to remember that myself. One thing for sure . . . it beats slinging salami!

As I go through the day, I will think of which unique strengths I contribute to my job. I will be enthusiastic about my work and bring a "touch of glory" to all I do.

$\mathcal{A}$re we almost there? When are we gonna get there? How much longer is it? I have to go to the bathroom." It's the universal language of children on a long car trip. Kids have it a lot easier now, of course. They can put on headphones and listen to music, play a hand-held electronic game— some families even have televisions in their vans.

Maybe it's just the mellowing of years, but I'm glad we didn't have headphones and GameBoys when I was a kid. We didn't have much in the way of entertainment; I'd get carsick, so I couldn't read. Instead we would play word games and listen to Dad point out rock formations and explain the geology of the land as we drove by.

We had a 1963 Ford Fairlane station wagon, white with bright red interior. "White car outside, fire car inside," my little brother called it. We took trips to Wyoming to visit cousins and see Yellowstone; to Disneyland, back when it was surrounded by orange groves; and across the deserts of Utah to Kansas and Grandma's house.

There was no air conditioning, of course. Mom

wet towels and stuck them in the windows, and Dad kept a 50-pound block of ice in a Styrofoam cooler so we could suck on ice chips across the desert.

Aren't those wonderful memories? They are now, but I recall I was kind of miserable at the time. I really wish we'd had air conditioning. And, hey, maybe it would have been nice to listen to tapes on my own little Walkman.

But I wouldn't have known about those rock formations and the geology of the western states, or just how good an ice chip can taste when you're in a hot car.

I'll keep the memories I have, thanks.

My memories are precious because they belong to me. Today, I'll take a minute to reflect on something pleasant from my childhood.

> *We must face what we fear; that is the case*
> *of the core of the restoration of health.*
> —*Max Lerner*

remember when I got my first real baseball glove on my ninth birthday in 1966. I had dropped numerous hints about what I wanted—a glove, a softball, and a bat. And on that glorious early summer morning, I flipped on the TV before I went to school. Captain Delta, the local cartoon host, always announced birthdays. Would he say happy birthday to me? Lo and behold, he did! And he told me to look under my bed, where there was a surprise from my mom and dad. I raced there immediately and found a real Spalding glove. It smelled wonderfully of fresh leather, and although it was a little big for my hand, I couldn't wait to play catch with Dad. My goal, you see, was to play in the Bobby Sox girls softball league.

There was only one problem: I was afraid of the ball. Dad would toss one easy, and I would turn away before I could see to catch it. "Just keep your eye on the ball," Dad said. "Put your glove up there—it won't hurt you if you catch it in your glove." I just couldn't shake the fear of getting smashed in the nose. I practiced and practiced, but I always flinched when it came at me.

That's also how I learned to handle conflict. For years, I would look away from a problem, rather than "follow it into the glove." Conflict threatened to smash me, and it was easier to flinch than face it.

I'm better at it now. Not perfect, but better. But it's taken a lot of practice to overcome my fear. I'm playing grown-up softball now, too. And I've made some pretty mean catches at first base.

Fear of being hurt can keep me from addressing conflict. I will look a problem straight on without flinching.

She was a woman of peace, of prayer, and of playfulness.

*T*got the call when I was in the middle of exams my junior year in college. "Grandma died yesterday." Dad's voice was shaky on the phone. This was the woman who raised him and his eight brothers and sisters on a Kansas farm, and a grandmother of forty.

I hadn't seen Grandma for several years—college and summer jobs had kept me away from the farm. Her funeral was an occasion for this large extended family to gather together, to tell stories and sing songs, to cry some, and to laugh a lot.

Laughing was something Grandma did often. At the funeral service, the priest who attended her in her last days talked about her ability to see the funny side of anything, and he told us a wonderful story that illustrated her character. Having fallen off the bed, Grandma lay there until the nurse happened to come in and notice her. Grandma's only question was "How did the floor get so close to my face?"

That was Grandma. The priest called her "a woman of prayer, of peace, and of playfulness." He'd known her only a short time, but as someone once said, people tend to die the same way they lived.

Do you ever wonder what people will say about you at your funeral? I would love it if someone said of me what was said of my grandmother. I can't think of a better way to be remembered.

What kinds of things do I want to be remembered for? Starting today, I will nurture the character qualities that I want to develop as I mature.

Lives of great men all remind us
We can make our lives sublime,
And, departing, leave behind us
Footsteps on the sands of time.
—Henry Wadsworth Longfellow

About five years ago, I got in line at an automatic cash machine. Taking my place behind the man in line, I caught a whiff of his scent. He smelled just like my grandfather! That scent took me back to the summers when we visited Grandpa and Grandma at the farm, rode the tractors, walked through wheat fields, helped milk cows, and chased prairie dogs in the truck.

But here I was, at a suburban bank, waiting in line for a machine that my grandfather could never have imagined. A machine that gives you money? Grandpa would have clucked his tongue and said, "Wow!"

All those thoughts raced through my mind as I stood behind this man who had the waffled, leathery neck of one who'd spent his life behind the wheel of a tractor. His white hair was cropped short under a feed cap, and he wore his shirt buttoned all the way to the top, just like Grandpa.

And that wonderful smell—it was sweet alfalfa and tractor grease, honest sweat and cow manure, all mixed together in a way that still says "Grandpa" to me.

I stood there at the cash machine, frozen in time. For a moment, I wasn't a grown-up anymore—I was six years old, on Grandpa's knee. I never saw the man's face, but I'm sure it was kind. I wanted to hug him and thank him for bringing back the memory of a man who's been gone for twenty years.

 As I remember special people who are no longer with me, I thank you, Lord, for the memories and the positive imprint they left on my life.

He ate and drank the precious words,
His spirit grew robust:
He knew no more that he was poor,
Nor that his frame was dust.
He danced along the dingy days,
And this bequest of wings
Was but a book. What liberty
a loosened spirit brings.

—*Emily Dickinson*

Take a walk on the beach on a summer day and what will you find? People stretching out on towels, sitting easy in low chairs, leaning against a cooler. Reading magazines, newspapers, paperback novels, letting the mind take a trip to somewhere else while the sun warms body and soul.

School kids have summer reading lists. While some lose themselves in the pleasure of reading, others are barely able to stay awake, and probably more than half wish they were playing ball instead of reading.

I'm continually torn between the two myself. To celebrate the season, I need to be outside, spending leisure time playing in water somewhere, hiking through the hills, or throwing a ball. But I also love the places that a good book can take me, and I can easily spend an entire summer afternoon in a rocking chair, feet propped up on the porch railing, lost in Faulkner's Mississippi or Conroy's South Carolina coast, Frederick Buechner's Bermuda or Flannery O'Connor's Georgia.

Those who are the least bit introspective or concerned about personal growth are tempted to confine their reading to practical, "self-help" books. But if you're willing to stretch your mind and use that imagination, you can learn a great deal about human nature—especially your own—from a well-written novel or short story. A good book can help you "dance along the dingy days," as Emily Dickinson would say.

I want to stretch my mind and use my imagination. This week, I'll find a good novel and take some time to read.

As a white candle in a holy place,
So is the beauty of an aged face.
—Joseph Campbell

*W*e live in a culture that reveres its youth and ignores its elders. Nearly every other culture does the opposite and is the richer for it. We are the poorer for having put our grandparents in retirement villages, far away from grandchildren who don't know the wisdom they are missing by not having Grandpa and Grandma around.

The things we can learn from our elders are limitless. They were born in a time that was very different from our own, and their perspective on life can be of great value as we struggle with our daily lives in this fast-paced, unsettling era. Imagine for a moment: A person born at the end of the last century would have lived through the First World War, the Great Depression, yet another World War, and the suburbanization of America. A telephone would have been a rare thing in the home of their childhood; now their grandchildren can have phones in their cars, their purses, and their pockets.

Life has changed at a speed never seen before in human history. More than ever, we need the sagacity of those who lived in a slower time.

Are the elders all gone from your life? Look

around—people who have lived rich, full lives are sitting near you in a pew, at the train station, and in a nursing home. Ask them questions. Listen, really listen, to their answers. Let them teach you with their stories.

I will listen to the wisdom of the elders around me, and remember the ones who have gone.

The heavens declare the glory of God;
And the firmament shows His handiwork.
—Psalm 19:1

*I*s there any better time of year than summer to go stargazing? Warm nights, crickets chirping, honeysuckle in the breeze, and a big black sky full of stars. You can lie on a blanket on the lawn or in the sand at the ocean or under your sleeping bag on a backpacking trip in the mountains. And to think that on any given night you and I are seeing the same stars—the Big Dipper, Orion, the Pleiades. I can't imagine that anyone could spend a night under the stars and not consider that there might be someone bigger than us, who somehow tossed these diamonds about the heavens. I like what the philosopher Immanuel Kant had to say. "Two things fill the mind with ever new and increasing wonder and awe—the starry heavens above me and the moral law within me."

The stars have inspired Kant, Shakespeare, Van Gogh—what great artist, writer, or poet hasn't used the stars as a subject? Children, lovers, astronomers, and singers find delight in the stars. What about you?

When was the last time you gazed into the night sky? The psalmist states that the heavens declare

God's glory. Want a wonderful way to contemplate the infinite? Brush up on constellations, take a child outside one night, and show him or her the wonder. "Up above the world so high, like a diamond in the sky . . ." I think you know the rest.

I will look up in the sky tonight and enjoy the wonder of the heavens.

*The art of leisure lies, to me, in the power
of absorbing without effort the spirit of
one's surroundings; to look, without
speculation, at the sky and sea; to become
part of a green plain; to rejoice, with a
tranquil mind, in the feast of colour in a
bed of flowers.*

—*Dion Calthrop*

*I*f summer is good for anything, it's for developing the art of leisure. These days, leisure is defined as what we do in our spare time, when we're not at work. That can mean anything from mowing the lawn to fixing the car to playing a competitive game of tennis.

All of those things are worthwhile. Mowing the lawn can be relaxing and even fun—so can puttering around under the hood of a car. Working up a good sweat is good for you, whether it's on the tennis court, in the gym, or on the running track.

But what about the fine art of doing nothing? I remember a poster in one of my high school classrooms: "When I work, I work hard; When I sit, I sit loose; When I think, I fall asleep."

I like that philosophy. It implies a healthy approach to life and leisure. Too many of us know good and well how to work hard—we've got the workaholic thing down to a science. Sitting is another thing entirely. Most of us are top-notch pros at "sittin' tight," but "sittin' loose" is not a practiced art.

Maybe it should be. Can you learn to "absorb without effort" the spirit of your surroundings? Can you look at the sky and sea and just enjoy them? Can you let yourself become a part of the scenery without thinking about every little thing that went on at work or at home yesterday? That would be a fine art to learn this summer.

I will develop the art of leisure in a way that frees me from being competitive or task oriented.

> *I am tired of four walls and a ceiling;*
> *I have need of the grass.*
> —*Richard Hovey*

One of the finest smells of summer, in my book, is the aroma of new-mown grass. Saturday mornings in June, my windows are open and I hear the familiar drone of a power mower.

Depending on how early it is, and how loud the mower, one of my favorite things is going back to sleep to the hum of that engine. Then, when I finally drag myself out of bed and start the coffee, I walk out on my front porch and catch a whiff of that freshly cut lawn. Ahhh, summer!

Oh, sure. You're thinking that I love the smell of grass because I don't have to mow it! I'd think differently if I had to do it myself every week or so.

Maybe. I guess I missed out on that chore growing up. Not because I was a girl; no, I did mow the grass. It's just that we didn't have very much of it in our California suburb where land was at a premium.

That's why I love mowing my friend's lawn. It's a third of an acre, I guess, and he has a cute little riding mower that goes pretty fast. I pretend to be Parnelli Jones on the Indy track, or a wheat farmer on a combine harvesting the grain. I have a great time and it's therapeutic. It amazes me, though, how quickly the grass grows between mowings in the summer. My friend Doug calls more frequently then. "Come on out for some therapy!" I'm glad to do it; it's fun for me, and it frees Doug to spend time with his kids.

Yes, I have need for grass. How about you?

Instead of complaining about a summer chore, I will find a way to enjoy it and have fun.

I have this big, hungry heart, you see, and nothing here is going to fill it to complete satisfaction. But . . . there are gifts from heaven: dear friends, hot coffee, good books, lightning bugs, watermelon, old houses, and music. And love, always love.

*T*wrote that in my journal on a day when I was feeling particularly lonely for no one in particular, except for God himself, perhaps. I imagine you have felt those same longings, to know and be known in a way that would touch the deepest places in your soul, those places only you have knowledge of. At times like that, the aching goes so deep that nothing seems to fill it—though we try, don't we? Sometimes the things we use to ease the hunger are destructive, like overindulging in food or alcohol or sex. Other things are more innocuous—spending money or watching TV. Even things that seem to be positive or for the good of someone else can be negative under the surface. We can suck our friends dry or demand more attention from our spouses while it appears that we are doing something for them. It's insidious, really. How can we be sure that our motives are pure?

We can't. But if we are able to recognize the hunger within us for intimacy and love, and realize that it may never be filled completely this side of heaven, then we can be free to enjoy the gifts we do have here—simple things like good books, good friends, and hot coffee.

Father, help me to keep from filling my spiritual emptiness with things that don't satisfy. I will enjoy life's simplest pleasures, knowing that they are gifts from above.

My advice to you is not to enquire why or whether, but just to enjoy your ice cream while it is on your plate, that's my philosophy.

—Thornton Wilder

*W*arning: this page may cause you to drop what you're doing, desert your responsibilities, and head for the nearest soda shop. I am writing in praise of ice cream, that ambrosia of the gods, that supreme delight of summer. Dripping from a cone, served in a paper cup or a crystal goblet, purchased from a street vendor, or received as a reward, there is nothing like the feel and taste of that creamy, cold concoction for bringing a smile to someone's face.

I was raised to believe that ice cream could cure anything, and I have no reason to doubt that. Whether it was a sore finger, an upset stomach, or a broken heart, Dad's remedy was always a milkshake. Sometimes he'd make it himself by throwing scoops in a blender, or he'd just put some in a glass with cold milk and a spoon and do some vigorous stirring. If the situation was serious, he'd take me down to the Fosters Freeze, where we'd share a chunky pineapple shake in two waxy paper cups.

That might have had something to do with my crush on a scooper at Baskin-Robbins. The summer of my sixteenth year, I spent fifty-five cents every single day just to get one of his extra-thick jamoca milkshakes. Nothing ever came of the romance, but I've never lost my deep, abiding love for ice cream. Now, if you'll excuse me, I've got to get to the Dairy Queen before it closes.

 Today, I'm going to put a smile on somebody's face and buy them an ice cream. Maybe even me.

> *Each friend represents a world in us, a*
> *world possibly not born until they arrive,*
> *and it is only by this meeting that a new*
> *world is born.*
>
> —*Anaïs Nin*

What a lovely thought! By the time we're adults, most of us have made so many friends that we have a universe of worlds that enrich our lives, interweaving and creating a prism of relationships that bring lovely colors and patterns to our lives.

It's not often that we take the time to consider the building blocks of relationships, or the things that a particular friend brings to our lives.

And think of all the other people you now care about, because they are important to your friend. Our friendship worlds expand exponentially as we grow in relationships, as their friends become ours.

Wonderful, isn't it?

I will take stock of my closest of
friendships, and be thankful for the
worlds I have known because of them.

As imperceptibly as Grief
The Summer lapsed away . . .
And thus, without a Wing
Or service of a Keel
Our Summer made her light escape
Into the Beautiful.
                                    —*Emily Dickinson*

I dread this time of year, as summer draws to a close. It starts with the back-to-school ads in the newspapers, and soon the high school bands are practicing in the afternoon. And though the heat of summer may wear on through October in some parts of the country, Labor Day weekend is the traditional end of the vacation season.

I hate it. School is back in session (a certain relief for many parents!). Although my life doesn't change just because school starts, I feel that familiar sense of summer's end. Playtime is over; time to go back to work.

I don't want to! Don't make me! I want summer to last and last. I want to take another trip to the beach, another spin around the lake, one more dive in the pool. I want to stay in my shorts and T-shirts, and I don't want to get my cool weather clothes out of storage just yet. I haven't finished my summer reading list! I didn't perfect my golf swing or my tennis game. I didn't visit my family enough. I didn't eat enough ice cream or drink enough lemonade or spit as many watermelon seeds as I wanted to.

Summer is always too short for me. But I'll let it go, eventually, and embrace once again the particular pleasures of fall. I'm just glad I had one more summer, aren't you? I'll carry its memories with me into the next season.

Knowing that summer is coming to a close, I will cherish the times I enjoyed with family and friends.

AUTUMN

a time to harvest

For Chuck and Debbie,
who showed me how
precious life is.

In the other gardens
  And all up the vale,
From the autumn bonfires
  See the smoke trail!

Pleasant summer over
  And all the summer flowers,
The red fire blazes,
  The gray smoke towers.

Sing a song of seasons!
  Something bright in all!
Flowers in the summer,
  Fires in the fall!

—Robert Louis Stevenson,
Autumn Fires

I grew up in a small town in the southwest that held a fiesta each September. A ceremony to "burn away" troubles kicked off the festivities. On Friday night, thousands of cars joined together on the high school football field to watch the burning of Zozobra—Old Man Gloom.

Zozobra was a huge cloth and paper dummy with a frightening papier-mâché head. His burning signified the end to all sadness for the fiesta period. I remember sitting on my family's car, watching Zozobra move his horrible head and long skeletal arms. At his feet, a fire-dancer jumped and leapt, waving two flaming sticks. The dancer ignited Old Man Gloom at the climax of the dance. Huge crimson flames shot into the air as Zozobra burned.

In a matter of minutes, blackened wire and glowing scraps were all that remained. Old Man Gloom was gone for another year; we could all be happy.

Friends of mine now practice a similar rite during autumn with a bonfire party. They ask their guests to bring whatever they wish to get rid of. Tax returns, bills, and leftover scraps from home remodeling projects are among the items flung into the flames.

Autumn is the perfect time of year to "burn away" our worries and problems from the past and start with a clean slate.

Today, I will leave my troubles and hardships behind where they belong, in the past.

Without dark, there is light. Without light, there is dark.

Fall brings cold, crisp mornings followed by warm, almost hot, days; black nights and bright days. Thus, it is a season of contrasts.

Contrast is necessary in our physical world because it's the only way we can perceive differences. An artist knows the benefit of black and white placed side by side on the canvas—the contrast makes the image more powerful.

Wouldn't it be wonderful if we could also tell differences so plainly in our own lives? We would know when we were in dark or light. It's possible.

There was a time, not too long ago, when I was trapped in the "gray"—the in-between. My life was "dullsville." Everything felt cloudy. I even went skiing (a favorite recreation) with close friends, but I didn't have a good time. The light had truly gone out of my life.

Luckily for me, a friend noticed something was amiss. She mentioned it to me. I shrugged my shoulders and said, "I dunno, I just feel off-base."

"So what are you doing about it?" she asked.

"Nothing," I said (which was the tact I was using for most everything during this time). "I'm hoping it'll go away on its own."

But it didn't. Things got worse. I teetered on the brink of depression; I had fallen into the dark. It was then that I asked for help—from this friend and from God.

God brought back the light to my life. I relearned a valuable lesson: I must first feel the light inside, through a close, personal relationship with God, before I can feel any light outside.

God, thank you for the light you bring to my life and thank you for the dark that is present so that I might know the difference between the two and know where I want to be.

Tis the last rose of summer
Left blooming alone;
All her lovely companions
Are faded and gone;
No flower of her kindred,
No rosebud is nigh,
To reflect back her blushes,
Or give sigh for sigh.

— *Thomas Moore*

*A*s the last blooms of summer fade away, frolicking children return to the classrooms leaving the neighborhoods silent and empty. No other event more exemplifies the contrasting nature of our feelings during autumn. On one hand we are happy to see our children go, ecstatic for the free time, but we are also saddened by their absence. This is particularly true when the last child starts school for the first time.

A close friend's youngest child starts kindergarten this fall, and she has mixed feelings. "I'm glad to finally have the free time to do things without being tied down," she says. "But I feel lonely, too, because he's my last child, my baby, and he's growing up."

We all experience good and bad feelings; it's part of human nature. But society wants us to disregard or "get over" bad, negative feelings. This is how our problems start—when we ignore our negative emotions.

The healthiest way to handle mixed emotions is to accept them. My friend plans to fill up her time with activities she's always wanted to do and to maximize the time she has with her child doing one-on-one activities. She also knows there may be rough times when she's depressed and lonely. These emotions are natural, a part of being human. It's what happens when things change.

Give me the strength to experience all of my emotions, positive as well as negative. Give me the foresight to learn from my feelings and to seek help when they become overwhelming.

*And He said, "The kingdom of God is as
if a man should scatter seed on the ground,
and should sleep by night and rise by day,
and the seed should sprout and grow, he
himself does not know how. For the earth
yields crops by itself: first the blade, then
the head, after that the full grain in the
head. But when the grain ripens,
immediately he puts in the sickle,
because the harvest has come."*

—Mark 4:26–29

*L*abor and celebration are two traditional activities of the harvest season. First, the field workers toil to bring in the harvest when the fruit, vegetable, or grain has ripened. Then, everyone revels in the bounty of that harvest.

Ancient customs celebrating the harvest season have included parties, dances, fertility ceremonies, and feasts. Many of these practices have dwindled since the 19th century, but such cultures as the Pennsylvania Dutch and some Native Americans still repeat the sacred rites of harvest.

In nearly all religions and cultures a strong correlation exists between the earthly harvest and the spiritual one. The reaping of the soul is no less crucial than the reaping of the wheat. It also requires labor and celebration. For as a seed thrown on bare ground and denied food, water, or sunshine will perish, so will the seed of love, planted deep within our hearts at birth, perish without care and nurturing.

Today, I will nurture the seed of love in my heart, so that I, too, may share in the great harvest celebration of my soul.

November's sky is chill and drear,
November's leaf is red and sear.
—Sir Walter Scott, Marmion

*A*nyone who is familiar with colorizing—the process of matching an individual's natural coloring with a season of nature—knows that fall is representative of warm colors. Red, orange, yellow, and brown are predominant fall colors. They are called "warm" because of the emotions one feels when around these colors.

Red represents passionate feelings, including love, anger, and danger. Orange emanates warmth and energy. And yellow gives off sunny, bright messages. All of these colors communicate with the subconscious, intuitive mind.

During the fall, colors send subconscious messages that make us feel loving, warm, and alive. We find harmony with ourselves and the world if we are attuned to the messages sent by the colors of the season.

Today, I will notice the colors that nature displays at this time of the year, and I will enjoy the effect they have on me.

A flower can bloom only if it's been nurtured along the way.

A colleague of mine is an avid gardener. She works her flower beds, meticulously digging up her dahlia bulbs and planting tulip and daffodil bulbs for the spring. The bulbs she plants in the fall are fertilized, the soil loosened and reworked. Dahlia bulbs require extra care to ensure they won't perish over the winter. They are dug up, hosed off, and packed away in sawdust for the winter, safe from freezing temperatures and rodents' sharp teeth.

This woman nurtures her bulbs with special care, for without it they won't bloom next spring. She's also an expert at nurturing her family. She ensures they have a clean home, good food, clothes to wear, and lots of fun activities. But this woman has no time left over to nurture herself. Without this nurturing, her personal blooms will soon wilt and die.

It's a sad fact that many of us treat ourselves much worse than we treat others. This is particularly true for women because the nurturing image has been instilled in us since birth. Self-nurturing is crucial, for only by nurturing ourselves can we even begin to nurture others. Find something to do today for yourself—take a walk alone, enjoy a long bath, read a good book. Look in the mirror and tell your reflection how proud you are of yourself and how much you love yourself.

 Today, I will find the time to take care of my own needs.

Like the cold of snow in time of harvest
Is a faithful messenger to those who send
him,
For he refreshes the soul of his masters.
—Proverbs 25:13

I met my neighbor at the park late one fall afternoon. He seemed so jubilant that I had to ask why.

"What a day!" he said. "My assistant called in sick. The boss reprimanded me for an unhappy client. Traffic was backed up all the way home."

"And you can smile?" I asked.

He grimaced. "Well, when I got home, I kissed my two children and wife hello, but my thoughts were still on the horrible day at the office. Luckily, my wife immediately noticed something was wrong. 'Take a walk,' she said. 'You look like you need a break. I'll explain it to the the kids.' So I did, and that's why I'm smiling. I feel a thousand times better now."

Perhaps some of us can relate to this man's experience. But how many of us have had this outcome? The more common scenario is to arrive home after a rough day and spend the rest of the evening in a daze, mulling over the day's unhappy events.

We should all be so fortunate to have a perceptive partner, as this man does. She was the fresh air he needed that day. He desperately required that time alone to clear his mind of his troubles.

When we are lucky enough to have someone who seems connected and empathetic to our feelings and needs, the effect is much like the refreshing, invigorating first frost of autumn. And the message seems just as clear as if it came from God himself.

Give me the clarity to be sensitive to another's needs and feelings today.

Boys and girls come out to play,
The moon doth shine as bright as day.
—18th Century Nursery Rhyme

The full moon closest to the first day of fall is dubbed the harvest moon. The harvest moon gets its name because of the additional light it gives farmers trying to win the race against the first frost. And, for reasons known mainly to astronomers, it is larger and brighter than most other full moons.

There's a different feel to the moon during the fall. The harvest moon is revered, even welcomed, for the extra light it gives when daylight is dwindling, and for the significance it carries for a bountiful harvest and future.

If I'm fortunate enough to see the harvest moon, I'll bundle up and take a walk. I am always awed by the moonlit landscape and the moonshadows. The air feels refreshing and invigorating—almost magical. This experience, when shared with a friend or a child, is very special.

When I see the harvest moon this fall, I will imagine it is a sign of good things to come.

Give us this day our daily bread.
—Matthew 6:11

I can't think of anything more comforting than the smell of baked bread. In fact, realtors suggest that clients bake a loaf to create a homey atmosphere while their house is being shown.

Bread baking is an art, and can be therapeutic as well. Kneading the dough is similar to throwing a pot on a potter's wheel—it makes one more aware of one's inner self or center. Just as clay has to be kept in the center of the wheel so the pot will be symmetrical, we, too, have to be centered in our own lives to keep from becoming off-balance.

Most days I feel about as centered as a skater on the end of a "crack-the-whip" line. I'm tugged from all angles—by the needs of my children, the wants of my husband, the desires of the PTA or the Scouts or the school, and the demands of my career. Sometimes I'm jerked around so much that I feel I'll crash into a wall.

I crave activities that help me get back to my center when my life gets this harried. One of those activities is making bread (not with the new bread machines, though—the old way, by hand). I love to grab a spongy handful of dough and push and pound out my frustrations. Eventually, the repetitious kneading slows the constant parade of thoughts through my mind and brings me back to my center.

I will do some activity today that makes me feel more centered and balanced.

How far that little candle throws his beams!
So shines a good deed in a naughty world.
—Shakespeare, The Merchant of Venice

During autumn, days grow shorter and nights grow longer. I'm particularly sensitive to the lack of natural light, so the increasing darkness that comes with fall depresses me.

While today we can quickly shut out the dark with a simple flip of the switch, we forget that a nearly perfect, low-cost source of light comes from a candle. A few photographers even choose candlelight over harsh incandescent or fluorescent lighting because it's softer and more becoming to their subjects. Legend purports that Abraham Lincoln did his schoolwork by candlelight.

A candle is a symbol of reverence and ritual. Some groups, such as Girl Scouts U.S.A., incorporate candlelighting into their ceremonies. A lit candle represents spiritual illumination and consciousness. Even today, many people meditate by candlelight. One need only to stare at the wavering flame to see how mesmerizing it can be.

Candlelight draws us back in time to a source of light used for thousands of autumns. As night cloaks the world in darkness and the fall wind whips up the leaves, I love to plan a candlelight dinner. My family thinks it's great and we save energy, too. Sometimes, we even pretend we're living in a time when candles were the only source of light.

Tonight, I will have a candlelight dinner to brighten up a dark autumn night.

When it's dark outside, I can feel the sunshine inside.

A telltale sign of autumn in the southwestern United States is strings of red chilies, called "ristras," hanging in front of white stucco homes. The chilies ripen into a deep red color in late fall, are picked, and then hand-strung. Outside, they dry and are preserved for the winter as seasonings for the spicy dishes of this part of the world.

An ancient Native American legend tells how the coyote grumbled to the Goddess of Seasons about the cold and dark winter. Seeing his point, she instructed him to grind chilies into a fine powder. He tasted the powder, and immediately felt the warmth of the sun on his tongue. He no longer felt cold. Later, people learned to make ristras for the same purpose.

I love to cook Mexican food when it's dark and dreary outside. As I taste the hot, spicy flavors, I recall the legend, and I remember sunny days at the beach, walks in the desert, and the feel of the hot summer sun on my face.

Lord, thank you for the things that bring memories of sunnier days.

> *. . . To set budding more,*
> *And still more, later flowers for the bees,*
> *Until they think warm days will never*
> *   cease,*
> *For Summer has o'er-brimm'd their*
> *   clammy cells.*
>
> *—John Keats,* To Autumn

I enrolled in field botany one fall quarter in college. Anyone who has taken a class similar to this knows one of the requisites is a field collection of flowers. *Great,* I thought. *Instead of writing a term paper, I get credit for picking flowers.*

Needless to say, I worked harder on that field collection than any other class that fall. Nearly every flower I found was of the immense and diverse family of sunflowers or asters. There are hundreds of species of asters. To make matters even worse, each flower head is made up of hundreds of tiny, individual flowers. And, it's those minuscule individual flowers that have to be dissected and recorded.

Sunflower heads are usually crawling with bees and other insects, ensuring more sunflowers to color our world and honey to enjoy. Roadsides are lined with asters and sunflowers during the fall. This fall, take a moment to really look at a sunflower; touch its center (watch out for the bees!); see if you can discern all the tiny flowers. It's fascinating how something so simple-looking to the naked eye can actually be so complex—another of God's incredibly intricate creations.

Thank you, God, for the beauty you bring to the earth during autumn.

*And let us not grow weary while doing
good, for in due season we shall reap if we
do not lose heart.*

—*Galatians 6:9*

*R*ecently I had one of those nights we all like
to forget. Dirty clothes littered the hallway. Screaming and yelling reverberated off the walls. *What's
wrong with this picture?* I asked myself. *Here I am with
the laundry and the kids while my husband's wining and
dining out of town on a business trip.*

I sighed and walked through the bathroom door-
way to referee another fight. An hour later, after
lots of cajoling, I had the kids seated on the couch
and ready for a bedtime story. I glanced at the
clock—only thirty minutes until bedtime and, finally, some peace and quiet.

"Mommy," my youngest daughter said.

"What?" I asked.

"I love you."

My other daughter chimed in. "I love you, too,
Mommy," she said.

My eyes filled with tears. I hugged both girls and
murmured, "I love you." Then I said a silent prayer.

I'm sure every parent or caregiver experiences
these feelings over and over. The childcare tasks
seem endless and thankless, until that one moment
when we catch a glimpse of the fruits of our labor.

There is no career more important than that of raising our young. It's also the most difficult. The innocent little ones can try our patience to the extreme. Instead of reducing the labor, they increase the work exponentially.

No one ever said it would be easy on this earth. And if it were, if there were no challenges, what would drive us, make us learn, and help us grow?

Along with the spiritual harvest of our souls is the work that gets us to that point. Possibly, it is the hardest work we will ever do; the most difficult to stick with. God promises: If we persevere, we will be rewarded. He shows us this in small ways (if we will notice) as he did for me on that night not too long ago.

I will look for God's handiwork in even the most menial task today, and be grateful for this life he has given me and for loved ones he has surrounded me with.

> *If you grieve for the dead, morn also for those who are born into the world; for as the one thing is of nature, so is the other too of nature.*
>
> —*St. John Chrysostom*

*F*all is a time of endings and beginnings. In the span of two months, a close friend of mine came face to face with birth as well as with death. One warm, sunny day in late September, her only daughter went into labor with her first child. Twenty hours later, my friend had a crinkly, red, newborn granddaughter.

The birth of any child is a miracle to behold, but there are few things more wonderful than the birth of a grandchild. My friend was ecstatic with this birth. There seemed to be new vitality to her outlook. Until she received the phone call in November.

Her mother died in her sleep. In a matter of hours, my friend's vitality dropped as she boarded a plane bound for California and the ensuing funeral.

Instead of joy and celebration, this woman felt emptiness and fear. She had lost the one person who brought her into this world. There was no longer the option to go home to Mom if her life's plans didn't work out.

My friend had much to resolve through the grieving process. But she also had much to be thankful for: a new granddaughter and memories from a lifetime of love from her mother.

Sages tell us that life and death are so closely related that we never understand until we pass over the line. God further instructs us that we have the opportunity to be connected to the afterlife through meditation and prayer.

The same joyous place that springs us into life at our birth calls us back upon our death. Thank you, Lord, for the opportunity you have given me to experience this joyous place while I am mortal.

*The harvest of our creativity can come
only when the mind is quiet.*

Don't you hate it when you really need to think clearly and your mind is muddled with all types of thought-clutter? It's sort of like a computer screaming an "insufficient disk space" error message. *Bleep,* we go on overload because of too much stuff crowding our brain waves. That's when it's time to take a break.

Brenda Ueland[1] recommended we all find idle time in each day. Rather than being non-productive, such time is actually the only way creativity will find an outlet. "So you see the imagination needs molding—long, inefficient, happy idling, dawdling and puttering," she says.

An artist needs such contemplation to see a vision; a writer, a storyline; and all of us, solutions to our problems. It's also the only way intuition can be heard, what some call communication from the unconscious mind.

If I can relax and calm my mind, I start to see solutions to some of my problems. When I dream, for instance, I get an idea that I would never have thought about during my waking hours.

Looking for ways to make idle time will help in calming our minds. Hobbies, such as cross-stitching, quilting, knitting, gardening, or wood-carving occupies our hands and slows down our thoughts. A famous mystery writer plays solitaire to help him plot and plan his books. I like to take a long walk each day. For me, it's a brief solace from my hectic day.

Today, I will find some time to be idle, to quiet my fast-paced life.

For so the LORD said to me,
"I will take My rest,
And I will look from My dwelling place
Like clear heat in sunshine,
Like a cloud of dew in the heat of harvest."
—*Isaiah 18:4*

*N*othing is more noticeable than fresh dew on a fall morning. It is a refreshing contrast to the dry, hot days of the harvest season. So distinct, in fact, that if it happens in the middle of the day, one couldn't miss it.

God's direction is much like that. If we are tuned in, we can actually see and hear his message very clearly, very distinctly. It's sort of like thinking of one's self as a radio receiver. The key is to tune in to God's frequency.

I know a couple who had a certain amount of money budgeted to purchase their first home. A real estate agent showed them a cute bungalow which had been on the market for some time. They each felt, intuitively, this was the one.

The husband felt he had a divine message from God directing him to offer a certain amount of money; no less, no more. So they phoned their agent with the offer. The agent was reluctant to forward the offer to the seller, but she did anyway.

Two hours later she phoned them back. "This sounds ludicrous, but the seller countered for $2,000 more than you offered. It's a great deal for that house."

The wife wanted to accept the contract, but her husband said, "No, I believe the Lord wanted me to pay this amount and that's our final offer."

The agent tried to persuade him otherwise, but he wouldn't waiver. One week later, the agent contacted the couple in person—the seller had accepted their offer!

God's direction is certainly not that clear in my life. But if it were, I know things would go a lot smoother.

God, give me the capability to hear your message as clearly as possible in my everyday life.

It's easier to focus on the one brown patch rather than the expanse of green lawn surrounding it.

I talked with a friend the other day. She told me that she and her husband just paid off their mortgage. I was amazed. Now that was an accomplishment!

"How did you celebrate?" I asked her.

"What do you mean?" she responded.

"Didn't you make a big deal out of it?"

"Not really. It was just another day."

We, as a society, don't celebrate enough. We certainly do enough complaining, though. You only have to watch the evening news or read the daily paper to see where our emphasis lies: on the pain, the negative, and the suffering.

It's important for us to look for small things, small accomplishments to celebrate. And if we can't find any of those, we can make some up. Some parenting books even recommend each person have one day (a week or month) designated as his or her special day. That person gets to choose what's for dinner and receives special treatment the entire day. You could even make a banner or have the person wear a crown. "Queen" or "King for a Day." Sounds hokey, but the person wearing the crown feels pretty good, especially if it's a young child.

It's a good idea to make a big deal of any small thing: getting the dog's shots, a good school paper, a clean house, or paying off a credit card.

I will find some small thing to celebrate today and make it a big thing.

You crown the year with Your
*   goodness,*
And Your paths drip with abundance.
They drop on the pastures of the
*   wilderness,*
And the little hills rejoice on every
*   side.*
The pastures are clothed with flocks;
The valleys also are covered with
*   grain;*
They shout for joy, they also sing.
*   —Psalm 65:11–13*

Autumn, for my grandmother, was the busiest time of year. She picked the fruit from the trees, harvested the vegetables, and spent hours in her kitchen over a steaming caldron, canning and preserving. The results of the harvest were on visual display in the rows and rows of canned green beans, tomatoes, peaches, jams, and jellies in her pantry.

I still do some canning and freezing in the fall, but the results of my labor over the past year are not on visual display like those jars in my grandmother's pantry. Anything that isn't visible isn't tangible. If I can't see the results, how can I be grateful? Did I accomplish anything this past year?

By the very act of living, I have made some mark on the earth, even if small—perhaps through my children, my husband, my friends, my occupation, or my church. Whatever the activity, there has been some accomplishment made this past year.

Take a piece of paper and write down all the wonderful things that happened to you over the past year. They don't have to be earth-shattering, either. In fact, it's the little accomplishments that really mean the most and for which we need to be proud.

I did this exercise because I found it hard to come up with any tangible accomplishments for our family. It was a very hard year for me and I was reluctant to revisit it. My oldest daughter had problems in school, my husband struggled with clinical depression, and I had an exhausting summer taking on the physical and emotional support of the family.

But as I forced myself to think of the year's high points, the accomplishments started to come to mind. Small, subtle things, like how my daughter got back on track and my husband and I entered counseling and my acceptance of our living situation, were actually major accomplishments. After doing this exercise, I saw how God had been working in my life over the past year. It humbled me that I hadn't noticed his work before.

I will be proud of all my accomplishments (minor and major) this past year, and grateful to God. If I can't think of any accomplishments, I will be grateful for simply making it through another year.

Offer to God thanksgiving,
And pay your vows to the Most High.
—Psalm 50:14

*I*n the United States and Canada we have a holiday set aside for the purpose of saying thanks for the year's fruitful harvest—Thanksgiving.

How much thanksgiving do you practice at other times of the year? If you're like me, very little, except, perhaps, at meals. (My children even fight over whose turn it is to say grace—a bone of contention that we are working on!)

Food is not the only thing to be thankful for, although it is an important gift. Our families, friends, homes, and material possessions are all blessings, too. And, most important, the fact that we wake up and can take another breath of life is reason enough to give thanks. Without this breath we wouldn't be alive and be able to enjoy the other things around us.

Do I really appreciate my life? Sometimes I look at my life as a burden—something I have to endure. This particularly seems the case when I'm experiencing powerful emotions or when I'm under stress, like the time I was late for an appointment, the phone kept ringing, and just as I got the kids out the door the dog soiled the rug. When things are bad it's hard for me to be grateful. My typical response is to wish things were different.

A little gratitude goes a long way. If I just close my eyes and say, "Thank you, Lord, for this life you have given me," I immediately feel better. And I think he does too.

 I will give thanks for my blessings each and every day.

The gift of life unwraps itself through time; all we need to do is sit back and enjoy its contents.

I watched my daughter unwrap a birthday gift addressed to her from her grandparents. She couldn't wait to open it and see what was inside. We are all enthralled with a present addressed to us. Most of the time, we don't care what's inside. The fun is the surprise element. But, if we have an expectation about what kind of gift we want, we're frequently disappointed by the contents. And we sometimes exchange it.

The gift of life is similar. It constantly unwraps itself and we experience what's inside. When we have expectations about our lives, we are usually disappointed by the way things turn out. When we're open to whatever happens, we are rewarded.

Lord, help me surrender and let my life unfold without expectation so I can enjoy your gift of life more fully.

Change and decay in all around I see;
O thou, who changest not, abide with me.
— *Henry Francis Lyte,* Abide with Me

*T*was hiking with my family one warm fall afternoon in the alpine meadows beneath Mount Rainier. The blueberries were ripe; the leaves bright red and orange. And there was a strange smell in the air.

"What's that odor?" a passerby asked me on the trail.

"It's the decaying vegetation," I answered.

He held his nose and walked on. Sure enough, most of the flowers, grasses, and shrubs were in the process of dropping leaves and dying back for the winter. Dead and decaying vegetative matter lay everywhere and a very pungent odor hung in the air. Unlike the gentleman who questioned me, I didn't find the smell distasteful.

Change and decay are facts of life in our world. We see them, smell them, feel them, and sometimes hear them, especially when the physical world changes around us as it does with the seasons. Nature depends on decay to survive. Without dying leaves, new leaves cannot come out in the spring. From decay springs change. And nature is based upon change.

Change can be disconcerting in our lives. A change of living area, change in family (by adding or subtracting a member), and a change of job all constitute life stressors. Too many changes can be disastrous, as my family found out firsthand. In the span of a few months we moved, changed jobs, and had a baby!

If the outside changes get too chaotic, I can always be with God inside my heart. It's the only place that never changes.

Only through change can I achieve my full potential.

*F*all signifies a period of physical change for the world between the flourishing period of summer and the languishing period of winter. Even though fall and winter are not normally thought of as times of growth, change by its very nature signifies growth. For example, without change a natural lake becomes eutrophic. A new source of water must enter and leave the lake to keep it from becoming stagnant.

The same principle applies to the world. What would happen if we were immersed in a constant season without change? In C. S. Lewis' *The Lion, the Witch and the Wardrobe,*[2] the fantasy world of Narnia was imprisoned by the White Witch in constant winter (a winter without Christmas to boot). The balance was upset and Narnia was in trouble.

Our lives can be like this sometimes. We avoid change because it brings risks of the unknown, which we fear. If we move to this place, what will happen? If we accept this promotion, will we be able to perform?

Change is stressful, no doubt about it. Too much

change can be detrimental. Too little change can also be detrimental. Some change is good.

Lord, let me embrace the changes that occur in my life as a necessary component to my growth and development.

He shall be like a tree
  Planted by the rivers of water,
That brings forth its fruit in its season,
  Whose leaf also shall not wither;
And whatever he does shall prosper.
                              —*Psalm 1:3*

*T*here are few things more delicious than the crisp sweet taste of a just-picked apple. I can remember going to the orchards as a child during the fall, after a long dusty ride over bumpy roads. Towering ladders leaned against trees laden with ripe apples. There were apples as yellow as tennis balls and as red as ripe tomatoes. We were given buckets and sent among the trees to pick as many as we could carry.

The good ones were always out of our reach. To the chagrin of my brothers, Mom wouldn't let us climb to the very top of the ladders. That was reserved for Dad. He always got the sweetest apples from the top.

Some we took home to eat, but we made cider in the creaking, wooden press with others. Dad would grind away on the handle as we threw in apple after apple. Chunks and stems flew everywhere. A worker helped us load the mash into the press, which would take three or four of us to crank.

The result was the finest cider we had ever tasted. We drank right out of the jug. Sometimes we would gulp down a whole gallon before we even got to the car. The cider we pressed ourselves always tasted better than the cider we bought from the orchard owners.

Sometimes I compare my life to those apples and the pressed cider from my childhood. When I strive and work hard, the rewards are plentiful and sweet. When I live my life actively, participating in decisions and actions, I feel better about myself, as if I'm a partner in my own destiny.

Today, I will approach my life actively, and make things happen. I will enjoy the results that come from my labor and efforts.

Who I am on the outside has nothing to do with who I am on the inside; who I am on the inside has everything to do with who I am on the outside.

When my friend's youngest child started kindergarten in the fall, she was left with an empty house and lots of time on her hands. For the first month she kept busy cleaning closets she never got to, filtering through old summer clothes, and fishing out winter garments. She even started to paint the interior of her home. And she was always there for the kids when they got home—a rarity in her neighborhood because most other women worked outside the home.

In mid-October my friend ran out of jobs to do, as well as the desire to do the jobs. She found herself drawn more and more to daytime television. Sometimes she wouldn't even get dressed until noon.

Her husband suggested she volunteer at the school, but that wasn't the answer. Something was missing from her life; something was wrong and she didn't know what it was. One morning my friend woke up and looked at herself in the bathroom mirror. "Who is this person?" she asked.

If we bank our identity on others or on our accomplishments (such as our career), we risk the loss of this identity when these things change or go away. And change they will!

God made us perfect in his image. We are entirely worthy in his eyes. All the other things we do while on this earth are merely what we do, not who we are. Our identity is who we are inside, not on the surface. We are children of God and, as such, worthwhile and loving persons.

My self-worth does not depend upon anything I do while in this world. Instead, my self-worth is firmly based upon God's unconditional acceptance and love.

Miracles occur when something is taken from its raw form and refined into something even better.

*C*ranberries are among many berries that ripen in the fall. I used to forage for cranberries along the shores of Lake Superior, collecting them from the small bushes that grew in the boggy cracks between the shoreline rocks.

Raw cranberries don't taste very good. They're mealy and sour. But baked in breads or muffins or cooked with sweeteners, cranberries have a unique flavor that many people enjoy.

This is an example of how a raw ingredient is improved with the processing done after it's harvested. A friend of mine feels the same way about himself.

"I look at myself as a lump of clay. Under God's guidance, I'm smoothed and shaped over time," he says. The challenge for us, this friend feels, is to remain flexible enough so that God can shape us.

It's not an easy challenge. I always know how I want my life to run; I must feel as mealy as a raw cranberry in God's hands. I wonder if he works harder on me or if he waits until I've softened, when I've given up or become vulnerable. I think it's the latter. Thus, it is to my benefit to be as flexible as possible, amenable to God's work in my life.

Lord, help me to remain open to your handiwork so that your divine hands can do miracles.

A child learns more by observing than by listening.

Autumn is usually the time of year when schools schedule open houses and parent-teacher conferences. My husband and I got a real jolt at our daughter's conference. Even though we constantly tell her about the value of school, she seems not to hear us. It's as if what we say goes in one ear and out the other. At one point, we even had her hearing checked.

Teachers and counselors agree that a child learns most effectively by example or doing. Lectures are the least productive means to teach anyone. The messages are always more effective if they're conveyed by actions.

That's been God's message to us from the beginning: Let your actions speak, not your words. This is why people readily condemn ministers and priests whose behavior is contrary to what they've preached. Hypocrites are not tolerated.

There are few of us who are not, in some way, hypocritical. I find myself lecturing my daughter to get her homework and chores done early, but this year I procrastinated filing my tax return and did it the night before it was due. When my daughter yells at me or her younger sister, I scream back, telling her not to yell. If I'm conscious of my actions, I'll stop myself and ask, *Is this the message I want to send to my children?*

Today I will be conscious of my actions. I know they will be more powerful than anything I might say.

Let your light so shine before men, that they may see your good works and glorify your Father in heaven.

—*Matthew 5:16*

A wise teacher once told me about his "light bulb theory." He said, "A light bulb does not have the words *light bulb* written all over it. If it did, no light could shine through all the letters. Instead, the light bulb just is. Its nature is to shine."

Have you ever noticed how moths, flies, and every other flying insects seem to flock to light bulbs? The saying "a moth to the flame" comes from this phenomenon. The same attraction exists for us human beings.

I've noticed I like to be around people who seem high on life and give off a type of light through their love. It feels good to be in their presence. Yet, these people don't lecture me or ask me to believe in their concepts or ideas. They just emit positive energy by their actions and behaviors.

Today, I will let my own light bulb shine.

If you eat a toadstool and don't die, it's a mushroom.

—*Anonymous*

Where I live, fall is known as mushroom season. Mushroom buyers flock to the backroads and sit in their trucks and vans, paying top dollar for gourmet wild mushrooms. If one knows one's mushrooms, one can make a bundle.

I have a friend who is a mushroom picker. I've gone picking with her on a few occasions, and it's amazing how similar all the varieties look to my untrained eye.

"This one is really poisonous," she says, pointing to a nondescript brown mushroom. "But this one is delicious." And she digs up one similar to the first.

The key to mushroom picking is knowing the differences between the poisonous and the edible varieties. For instance, sorrels have a solid, ridged undersurface rather than the fleshy folds of most other mushrooms. But that's not the only characteristic. A mushroom picker has to be an expert. To be otherwise is to toy with death.

Picking and choosing what the world offers isn't as graphic as a wrong mushroom choice, but it can sometimes be just as deadly. One only has to watch the evening news or read a newspaper to see how other human beings have gone wrong. Unfortunately, we're supposed to learn from others' mistakes, but that isn't easy. A better way to learn would be to have a diagnostic tool, much like a "mushroom key," that would point the way toward the right, healthy choices we must make. The Bible can be that key.

I will meditate on God's word and direction today as a key to help me make the right choices in my life.

Strange to see how a good dinner and
feasting reconciles everybody.
— *Samuel Pepys,* Diary

*H*uge feasts that celebrate the bountiful harvests have always been a ritual of the autumn season. Our Thanksgiving holiday finds its roots in this tradition.

In the Hawaiian culture, feasting is considered an opportunity to be close to God. The Hawaiians believe that food is a gift and, as such, should be appreciated with special reverence. A Hawaiian feast is an act of communion with God.

With shorter days and longer nights at this time of the year comes the opportunity for dining together with friends. And, whenever two human beings are communicating, God has found an avenue for his message.

At this time of year, I like to invite friends over for an impromptu dinner. If we are grateful for the blessings we received over the past year, the meal becomes fulfilling spiritually as well as physically.

I will make an opportunity for fellowship
by breaking bread with others today.

I have to be careful what I ask for because I might get it.

*H*ave you ever wanted something and then received it, although probably not in the way you expected? This happens frequently to me and it's unnerving.

In my business, peaks and valleys are the name of the game; feast or famine. I finished an intense project under a very tight deadline and looked forward to a time when my life wouldn't be so hectic.

After I met my deadline, I spent the next two weeks recovering, in a daze. It was as if I weren't inspired to write. (I've since talked with other writers and they tell me the same thing happens to them.)

I found myself secretly wishing for another project, something to motivate me. In a matter of weeks, my wishes came true. Whether I was ready or not, I was back against tight deadlines and lots of work.

Now that I look back on it, I realize God answered my request. I truly believe, with trust and patience, God answers our prayers in ways that are even better than we first imagine. I wonder if there's a part of us that instinctively knows what we need, when we need it, and how to obtain it (with God's help).

God is waiting to give us what we need. All we have to do is ask.

Trust in the LORD with all your heart,
And lean not on your own understanding;
In all your ways acknowledge Him,
And He shall direct your paths.
                                    —*Proverbs 3:5, 6*

*A*man I know had a hard time adjusting to
life after his divorce. He lived alone in an apartment. Nights and weekends were the most difficult.
In the beginning he watched a lot of televised sporting events. When that got boring, he visited the
neighborhood tavern, but soon grew tired of the
smoky, depressing atmosphere.

Many times he cried himself to sleep. He said it
never occurred to him to ask for help. For months
he tried to tough it out and get through the pain.

One night, when things got really bad, he stared
at the ceiling for a long time, feeling the hurt and
loneliness inside. The familiar tears started to roll
from the corners of his eyes.

A prayer he recalled from his childhood came to
mind: "The LORD is my shepherd; I shall not
want. . . ." (Psalm 23). He fell asleep mumbling the
words to himself. It was the most comforting sleep
he'd had in a long time.

Since then he has learned to ask for help. He
regularly turns to God for help and guidance. And

he also talks to others, such as those in the same predicament. While he doesn't feel he's recovered from the divorce, he knows he doesn't have to suffer alone.

Autumn is a time when many of us experience intense emotions. It's a time of change, and change affects our emotions. If I find myself suffering from sadness and depression and things get too negative for me to handle, I know I need to ask for help.

God stands ready to support us, to show us the way, and to hold our hands as we walk. The only catch is that we have to first ask for his help. God will help only those who solicit his guidance.

God cannot answer our cries for help unless we knock on his door. I will learn to ask for his help whenever I need it.

God's works are good. This truth to
   prove
Around the world I need not move;
I do it by the nearest pumpkin.
                    —*Jean de la Fontaine*

A pile of orange pumpkins in front of a fruit stand or grocery store is a symbol of fall. Roaming through a pumpkin patch to pick out that perfect specimen for a jack-o-lantern or pie is an activity enjoyed by thousands during the month of October.

God is omniscient, omnipresent, and omnipotent. Every object or living creature has the mark of God's hands on it. Everything was created by God and everything is connected by this common thread.

Sometimes we think of God's work only in majestic proportions—a mountain range or a cathedral or witnessing the miraculous recovery of a terminally ill patient. But evidence of God's presence can also be seen in a droplet of rain, a single snowflake, the first smile on a baby's face, and a small green shoot coming up through the snow.

Life vibrates in everything we hear, see, and smell in the world around us. God is everywhere—from the sun to the tiniest grain of sand. This is the miracle of creation for which we need to be grateful.

I will notice God's presence in everything I experience today.

> *Finally, brethren, whatever things are true,*
> *whatever things are noble, whatever things*
> *are just, whatever things are pure, whatever*
> *things are lovely, whatever things are of*
> *good report, if there be any virtue and if*
> *there is anything praiseworthy—meditate*
> *on these things.*
>
> *—Philippians 4:8*

*H*ave you ever noticed how good you feel when you're around people who seem enthused with life? I do. I don't think it's coincidence either. I believe God planned the world in such a way that we would feel good when around the beautiful, the pure, and the just. In fact, prophets tell us to look at our souls as if God programmed two very opposing feelings within every human being.

The first is called a "cup of joy." Whenever we drink from this cup we feel great, incredible, and happy. Things that surround us, such as our loved ones, the beauty of nature, and the miracle of creation, make us drink from this cup.

But God also gave us a "cup of sorrow." And He did so because this was the only way we could tell what the cup of joy tasted like. He arranged for the cup of joy to taste imminently better than the cup of sorrow, but we would never know that until we tasted the cup of sorrow.

Unfortunately, we have one problem: The human race has become hooked on the cup of sorrow. In fact, we're so preoccupied with how bad it tastes that it seems we have completely forgotten about the cup of joy.

Meditating on the good in the world, on the beautiful, the joyful, and the happy, will help us to rediscover our own cups of joy. If we redirect our focus to these things and contemplate them, we will be drinking from the cup of joy and be reminded how wonderful it is to be alive.

God, help me to find the "cup of joy" within myself and to drink freely of its nectar.

Laugh, and the world laughs with you;
Weep, and you weep alone,
For the sad old earth must borrow its
mirth,
But has trouble enough of its own.
—Ella Wheeler Wilcox, Solitude

*T*here's not enough humor in the world. When some of my friends start getting the autumn blues they play "Mad Dog," the game written about by Laura Ingalls Wilder.[3] First they turn off all the lights in the house and someone hides. The rest of the family look for that person. When they get close, the hidden person jumps out and screams. They end up running and laughing throughout the house. If tension is in the air and they find themselves at each other's throats, one of them says, "Let's play Mad Dog," and it always makes them laugh and feel better.

Laughter is one of the best ways to cope with and beat the effects of a stressful life. No matter how much pain or suffering we see, if there is a smile, a giggle, or a laugh, we know things are okay.

Laughter is contagious! It's the best thing we can give back to the world. And it's the finest medicine for ourselves. I find that if I look at some old photos or a school album, there's always something that makes me laugh. Think of something funny that happened to you once. Call up a friend. Better yet, rent or go to a funny movie, watch a comedy show on television, or play a humorous game with your family.

Today, I will find something to laugh about and share it with someone who is special to me.

> *No Spring, nor Summer beauty hath such*
> *grace,*
> *As I have seen in one Autumnal face.*
> *—John Donne,* The Autumnal

I grew up near my grandmother and my great-aunt. One was a widow, the other a spinster. As a child, I resented the time my mother made me spend with these two elderly ladies. It felt so stifling to be in their house when I longed to be outside in the fresh air with kids my own age. I'd fidget about until I could finally escape.

Now that I'm older and both my grandmother and great-aunt have long since died, I remember conversations with them far more vividly than my playtimes outside. I recall one instance in particular when my great-aunt told me about growing up in Germany. I watched her eyes light up and thought I saw a glow around her white hair. She looked beautiful.

Unlike other cultures, we have lost the valuable resource of our older society. We put them out of the way in nicely-packaged senior centers and nursing homes. Although these establishments provide the type of care which usually cannot be given elsewhere, by doing so we've lost a vast source of wisdom and experience. No wonder our children fear the aged—they are kept away from them. Many children, like my own, see their grandparents only a few days out of the year, if at all.

There are winds of hope, though. Some schools and daycare centers have tapped the senior population for help. It's great for those seniors who are interested, and even greater for the children.

Now is a prime opportunity to spend time with those in their autumn of life, to be in the presence of the grace that comes only after a lifetime of trials and joys.

Today I will seek out someone who is years ahead of me in life, either in person or by phone.

Praise the ripe field, not the green corn.
—*Irish proverb*

For most of my life I lived in the southwestern part of the United States. I always marvel at how cornfields seem to thrive in spite of the extreme climatic conditions of this region—long periods of scorching heat, cracked soils, and torrential rains.

Corn is sacred to Hopis, Navajos, and countless other societies, including the Mayan culture of Central and South America. It is considered a sustenance of body and soul and a necessary ingredient in ritual after ritual.

Corn, to a Hopi, is a reflection of the human life span. First, the seeds are planted in moist, tilled soil. The seed is nurtured, just as a Hopi child is nurtured. Everyone prays for the corn to grow, just as they pray for the children to grow.

With this careful attention the corn grows into green stalks reaching toward the immense blue sky. Under the blazing summer sun, the leaves wilt and close up, as a human does under the pressure of challenge. The rains come and, as if by magic, the corn rejuvenates, ready to reproduce. People do the same when showered with love and understanding.

The culmination of the cycle comes when the

corn is ready to be harvested. This is the fruit of the Hopis' labor and faith.

After the harvest, the old canes are pushed over and returned to the earth, as people are when their time is over. (In the Hopi language, the same word is used for spent corn and for a spent person.)

Each step in the process is crucial. Only through carelessness or lack of effort and spirit will the earth deny the Hopi its corn. The entire process requires intense faith and prayer to work. And as a result, the harvested corn is the mainstay of the Hopi society.

It would be wonderful to be as attuned to this seasonal cycle as the Hopi, living my life as a simple mirror of the life stages of a corn plant. Each step in the process from birth to death would be crucial, a building block for the next. Every stage would have an obvious purpose and I wouldn't feel so lost along the road of life. The tasks of childhood, adolescence, and adulthood would all lead to the ultimate harvest of my soul.

I know not when my own harvest will come, but I must prepare for it by tending my seed and nurturing my plant along the way.

For the ignorant, old age is as winter; for the learned, it is a harvest.

—*Jewish proverb*

A close friend of mine recently retired from her job after nearly thirty years of service. Her office held a retirement luncheon in her honor and presented her with a commendation and several nice gifts. "It was a nice send-off," she said.

The woman had been an outstanding, intelligent, and productive employee. Yet, by her fifty-fifth birthday she was no longer of use. Of course, it was her decision to leave, but she experienced what many retirees do today when her employment ceased—a loss of self-worth.

Our society's population pyramid is top-heavy. Our largest segment, the baby boomers, is approaching retirement in the next few decades. Not only is this going to be a financial drain on the country's retirement system (already a concern to legislators), but an entire generation will leave the business world. And so will the corresponding knowledge and experience.

Some companies are progressive enough to realize the value of their older, more experienced employees and have assigned them the task of training new employees. Unfortunately, this is a rarity. More common is the practice of reducing senior employees' responsibilities and putting them "out to pasture" in a job where they simply wait for retirement. Company policy interprets these employees as having passed beyond their productive and useful years. The wise person knows otherwise.

I will look to someone more experienced than I for wisdom; the resulting knowledge I gain will be invaluable.

Two halves brought together in marriage do not make a whole.

I was married one day in October and my life was forever changed. Marriage means different things to different people. A pastor friend of mine summed it up for me by saying, "Marriage is a process whereby a man and a woman are both inspired to reach higher plateaus than if they were alone. It's instant defeat if one looks to the marriage partner for satisfaction. One must approach the altar a whole person and through the marriage process, two whole persons become more effective together than apart."

We can apply these same principles to our daily lives. Our biggest lesson may just be that our fulfillment doesn't come from any outside source, be it another person or material possessions. Rather, our gratification comes from inside our hearts and through a personal relationship with our creator. Thus satisfied, we are then equipped to give back to the rest of the world.

God, help me to become a complete and fulfilled person through your love and acceptance.

When I'm not looking, I usually find it.

$\mathcal{I}$ have a friend who is an intelligent young woman. On the surface she has everything going for her—financial security and a rewarding career. Underneath, she's unhappy. She wants to marry and is on the lookout for the "right" guy. Other friends who know this woman are amazed no man has found her. They say, "She has everything going for her. Why hasn't she married?"

I'm sure there are other issues here, but I feel the reason this friend may not have found what she is looking for is because she's immersed in the search. I have another friend who wished she could find a husband. Interestingly enough, once she stopped wishing, she met the man she eventually married.

When we're not looking for something, we usually find it or, more accurately, it finds us. It works with objects as well. An instructor told me if you lose an object, you can use your intuition to find that object again by letting go of the search. (Of course, this is much more difficult if it's a set of car keys and I have to leave at a certain time. All the more reason I should keep an extra set available in such emergencies.)

Once I lost my favorite brooch. I spent weeks looking everywhere for it. Finally, I gave up. Less than one day later, I found the brooch pinned on a sweater.

 When I need something in my life, I trust it will be found at the right and perfect time.

Time is man-made.

A wise teacher once told me, "The past is a canceled check; the future a promissory note. The only real hard cash is in the present." Other sages preach that passion is in the moment; celebrate the temporary; take time to smell the roses. This advice is aimed at getting the human race to focus on the present.

In my life, I find myself preoccupied with the past and the future. *If only things had been different,* I think. *Maybe things will be better,* I wish. And in doing so, I am robbing myself of my only real asset—what is happening now.

Consider this: Our senses do not function in the past nor the future. We cannot see, smell, taste, hear, or feel something that has happened before or that will happen in the future. What we sense in the present may trigger a memory, but the sensation is happening in the present, not the past.

God gave us our senses as a means to experience his creation. Therefore, we are not intended to spend most of our waking hours focusing on a time when we cannot use these senses. Enjoying the sights, sounds, smells, feelings, and tastes of fall is

one of the best ways we can be truly in the present
and enjoy the riches of the moment.

*Lord, help me stay in the present by
reawakening me to the sensations I
receive from the world.*

You only go around once in life so why not enjoy the trip?

I am goal oriented, and I'm not alone. The majority of our society is trained from an early age to be this way. The measure of success is not how someone got to the top, but the fact that they are at the top—the end result. Being goal oriented is not bad, unless we focus so much on the goal that we miss the lessons necessary to reach that goal.

Peter Jenkins made a journey that ultimately changed his life.[4] Anyone who has read his books knows that his story does not focus on his goal— reaching the Pacific Ocean—but on the exciting and educating ventures he experienced en route. It was these interim adventures that changed his life. If the destination of his trip were more important than the journey, then he would have had no reason to write his books—and we would have no reason to read them.

For most of us the lesson is not learned at the end of the journey, but along the way. The *process* is when the magic occurs; the end result when the *applause* happens. Missing the magic and just witnessing the applause leaves us wondering what everyone is clapping about.

Today, I will enjoy the journey, the process that gets me to my goals.

*The world seems so unfair because we can't
see it through God's eyes.*

I have a friend who has been stricken with cancer. She's not very old and has a young, growing
family. It's a tragic set of circumstances. This
woman does not possess any of the high risk factors
for cancer. Until her diagnosis, she was an active,
healthy individual. Even her physicians shook their
heads.

I had the privilege of spending some time with my
friend recently and we talked about how priorities
change when one faces a life-threatening situation.
"I know it sounds crazy," she told me. "While I'm
not overjoyed to have this disease, I feel my life has
changed for the better. My friends and family have
all rallied around me and I have a new appreciation
for humanity that I don't think I would have, had
I not gotten cancer."

I'm not implying that God meant for this person
to have cancer. I can't even comprehend what God's
intentions are in this matter. And I want to shout,
"It's not fair! Why does this have to happen to her?
She never did anything wrong!"

Does God make mistakes? "Of course not,"
would be our vehement reply. But how many of us
really believe it? How many of us can understand

what happens in our crazy world and really feel it isn't a mistake?

The only thing I can do is accept and pray for that comprehension. If it doesn't come, at least I'm comforted in the knowledge that God is in control and he knows what he's doing.

I will try to accept my life as is (joys as well as sorrows) because I know God is in the pilot's seat and he knows how to fly this plane better than I.

> *The heavens declare the glory of God;*
> *And the firmament shows His*
> *handiwork.*
>
> *—Psalm 19:1*

*T*he heavens are a marvel to me. Surely, they are the finest example of God's handiwork. I spent one fall on the north shore of Lake Superior, far away from any cities. Here the night skies were breathtakingly beautiful. The stars seemed so bright, so close I could almost touch them. An added bonus was the frequent displays of northern lights. "The best in years," I was told by locals.

I was driving from Canada to Minnesota with a friend late one night when I saw my first aurora borealis. That experience remains etched in my mind. The northern lights are incredible to behold. No matter how descriptive one can be, no one knows what it's like until he or she has seen them firsthand.

My first thought upon viewing the display— pinks, purples, reds, greens—in the night sky was, *These aren't subtle at all. You can't miss the curtains of colors that fall from the heavens.* My second thought was, *It's a miracle!* And my third thought, *God can paint!*

When I look upon the night sky, I will see God's creativity in its display.

> *So Moses said to him, "As soon as I have*
> *gone out of the city, I will spread out my*
> *hands to the LORD; the thunder will cease,*
> *and there will be no more hail, that you*
> *may know that the earth is the LORD's."*
> —*Exodus 9:29*

*M*ountains surround the little town where I grew up. I remember waking up on fall mornings and seeing the mountains draped with a delicate fog that stood out against their purple-blue outlines. It happens only during the fall; the rest of the year the temperature isn't quite right for fog to form. I haven't been back to this town in years, so I don't know if the phenomenon still occurs or if there is too much smog obscuring the mountains.

My husband's grandmother lived in southern California until her death at age ninety-five. She saw a lot of changes in the Los Angeles area during her lifetime. The San Bernardino Mountains are very close to her home and she remembered being able to see them nearly every day. Not so anymore.

The global environmental crisis is hardly a surprise . . . it's a heated issue in politics and the daily news. Most of us acknowledge the world needs our help before it's too late, but we disagree who should shoulder the responsibility.

The air, soil, and water belong to the Lord and have been loaned to us while we're on the earth. We are stewards of this creation. It makes sense that we should take care of these gifts. Simply put, if we mess up our backyard, we need to clean it up or else it becomes unsafe to live in.

Cleanup doesn't have to be the responsibility of the government. A government is just a collection of people. Cleanup starts with each individual.

I will make a difference in my global environment by my individual actions today.

> *Seek in reading and thou shalt find in*
> *meditation; knock in prayer and it shall be*
> *opened to thee in contemplation.*
> —St. John of the Cross

*I*n the area I now live, fall is marked by dreary, rainy, gray days. Even the leaves seem to drop before their fall colors appear. It can get depressing.

Thus, I am forced to spend a lot of time indoors stoking the fire to keep dry and warm. The too-easy form of entertainment these days is the television. Fortunately (or unfortunately, depending on how I look at it), I have very limited television reception. But there's always a video to watch and, too often, my children resort to this on these rainy fall days.

When I pick up a book, however, I'm transported into a world of wonder and adventure. Reading is my passion. And I'm not alone. In fact, where I live there are more library cards per capita than anywhere else in the county.

Autumn can be a time for contemplating, a relief from the backbreaking pace of summer and its multitude of outdoor activities. One can slow down and enjoy the time indoors, nestled beneath a blanket in front of a roaring fire, safe and warm, while the weather creates havoc on the outside world.

What better time to read? Reading a good book

is one of the best forms of entertainment. It is not a mindless activity like watching television or movies, which has its worth if used properly. Reading is an interactive exercise, an opportunity to join the imaginary world the author has created and to be an active participant in an adventure without ever having to leave the couch. And reading aloud to children is a special way to share.

I will read a book today. It's one of the best ways I can exercise my imagination.

> *Therefore whoever hears these sayings of*
> *Mine, and does them, I will liken him to*
> *a wise man who built his house on the*
> *rock: and the rain descended, the floods*
> *came, and the winds blew and beat on that*
> *house; and it did not fall, for it was*
> *founded on the rock.*
>
> *—Matthew 7:24–25*

*A*utumn can be a time of violent weather—
a characteristic of the unstable patterns that this
transitional season brings. One late autumn weekend, a disastrous flood hit the northwestern part of
the United States. In a matter of hours, many people
were without homes and some had lost their lives.

Since that historic event the building codes for
this area have become more stringent. Building in
a floodplain is almost impossible and in marginal
flooding areas, very specific foundations have to be
constructed to allow for the movement of flood-
waters but still keep the structure anchored. Corre-
spondingly, building costs have escalated.

Several hymns praise the foundation the Lord
provides us in our own mortal lives. If we anchor
our existence in his teachings and promises, if we
have faith in God, we can survive anything—even
a life-threatening catastrophe because we know that

no matter what happens to our mortal bodies, our souls live on with God into eternity.

I will live my life firmly anchored in a belief in God, and that will be my strong foundation to hold me no matter what assails me.

> *While the earth remains, seedtime and*
> *harvest, cold and heat, winter and summer,*
> *and day and night shall not cease.*
> *—Genesis 8:22*

*G*od's covenant with Noah was a covenant with all human beings. The evidence of this promise (in God's words) is the changing seasons. God intends us to enjoy each season as it comes and, more importantly, embrace the seasons as a natural cycle of life on earth.

As autumn nears its end and winter looms on the threshold, change is in the air. Where I live, there's an extra chill in the morning air that wasn't there before. It doesn't warm up enough during the day to melt the frost. The vegetation turns black and gray. The leaves have dropped from the trees and stark branches reach toward a slate-gray sky.

A few birds still flit about, but the outdoor activity of the animals is quieter. A stillness seems to descend on the world. The flurry of preparation is done. The world seems poised, waiting for the coming winter and hoping it won't be too cruel.

As much as I love autumn, I look forward to winter. I know that fall can't occur year-round. I love autumn because it brings change to the world around me and because it provides contrasts in my life (vivid sensations outside, vivid memories and feelings inside). But I also love autumn because it brings winter.

I will look forward to the coming winter as a sign of God's promise to all living creatures.

NOTES

1. Brenda Ueland, *If You Want to Write* (St. Paul, MN: Graywolf Press, 1987).

2. C. S. Lewis, *The Lion, The Witch, and The Wardrobe* (New York, NY: Macmillian Publishing Company, Inc., 1978).

3. Laura Ingalls Wilder, *The Little House in the Big Woods: Little House on the Prairie* (New York, NY: Harper & Row, Publishers, 1960).

4. Peter Jenkins, *A Walk Across America II* (New York: William Morrow and Company, Inc., 1981).

ABOUT THE AUTHORS

Debra Klingsporn, author of *Winter,* is a freelance writer, editor, and marketing consultant. She has more than fifteen years of experience in publishing and communications, and is coauthor of *I Can't, God Can, I Think I'll Let Him.* Debra lives in Edina, Minnesota, with her husband, Gary, and their two daughters, Katy and Kari.

Anne Christian Buchanan, author of *Spring,* is a freelance writer, editor, and marketing consultant. She served as an in-house editor for Word, Inc., prior to starting her own editorial service business six years ago. Anne is coauthor of *I Can't, God Can, I Think I'll Let Him.* She lives in Knoxville, Tennessee with her husband, Stan, and daughter, Elizabeth.

Bernie Sheahan, author of *Summer,* is a writer and columnist for *Aspire, Release, Nashville Scene,* and travels the world on assignment for World Vision. She spends her summers reading the works of C.S. Lewis, Flannery O'Connor, and Pat Conroy. Bernie lives in Oxford, Mississippi, where she is working on a novel and pursuing a Masters degree in Southern Studies at the University of Mississippi.

Catharine Walkinshaw, author of *Autumn,* writes for both children and adults, and is the author of numerous articles and books. Her love of God and nature is shown through her prose. She holds a degree in biology and writing from the University of Colorado. Catharine resides near Mount Rainier National Park in Washington State with her husband, Eric, and two daughters, Alex and Camille.